ART EXHIBITION DOCUMENTATION IN LIBRARIES

Cataloguing Guidelines

Compiled by the
ARLIS/UK & Ireland Cataloguing and Classification Committee

ARLIS UK & IRELAND **Art Libraries Society**

2000

Extracts from the *Anglo-American Cataloguing Rules*, 2nd ed., 1998 revision are reprinted with permission of the copyright holders: the American Library Association, the Canadian Library Association and The Library Association.

Title pages in Part III reproduced courtesy of:

Annely Juda Fine Art
Djanogly Art Gallery
Fitzwilliam Museum
Royal College of Art
Royal Photographic Society
Tate Gallery Publications
University of Brighton
Whitworth Art Gallery

ISBN: 0 9519674 7 9

Printed in Great Britain by Titus Wilson & Son, Kent Works, Burneside Road, Kendal.

Art Exhibition Documentation in Libraries: Cataloguing Guidelines

Contents

Preface

These guidelines have been developed in response to a perceived need within the art library community. They are an attempt to achieve greater consistency in the application of the Anglo-American Cataloguing Rules to the cataloguing of exhibition documentation. They have been compiled by the ARLIS/UK & Ireland Cataloguing and Classification Committee; in particular by members of the exhibition catalogues subgroup comprising Nicola Hunt (Tate Gallery Library), Anne Sutherland (British Library), Jane Savidge (Central Saint Martins College of Art and Design) and Gerry White (National Art Library). The current work builds upon an earlier unpublished draft compiled by Dr. John Bowman, Marion Wilks and Jane Savidge under the auspices of the same ARLIS Committee chaired by Dr. Stephen Bury. This preliminary draft was distributed in 1987.

The task of developing the unpublished document as a publication was picked up by Gerry White, then incoming chair of the ARLIS Cataloguing & Classification Committee. Nicola Hunt and Anne Sutherland commenced the work of revision assisted by two further committee members, Elizabeth James (National Art Library) and Alison Felstead (Bodleian Library) who provided assistance and expertise. In June 1998, participants at an ARLIS Workshop on Cataloguing Exhibition Catalogues tested an early draft of the present document and discussed the problems and pitfalls of cataloguing exhibition catalogues. The evaluation provided by this workshop, assisted the revision process by suggesting further aspects for inclusion. Members of the ARLIS Publications Committee also provided helpful comments.

The guidelines presented here are based wherever possible on a consensus view. Where there are differences in the interpretation of AACR2 as applied by UK and US institutions these differences are noted. It is hoped that by identifying common ground and highlighting aspects which are treated in slightly different ways, we will help individual cataloguing agencies reach a better understanding of the issues involved. We hope that these guidelines will promote discussion and rule revision to reduce such differences in future.

Thanks are due to Sue Brown (Library Association) and to members of the Library Association/British Library Committee for the Revision of AACR2 for supporting work on the Guidelines at an early stage in their development.

Jane Savidge, Chair
ARLIS/UK & Ireland Cataloguing & Classification Committee

Art Exhibition Documentation in Libraries: Cataloguing Guidelines

1. Introduction

"The exhibition catalog, in all its forms, is an essential part of the art-historical food chain, providing factual data for the identification, dating and provenance of art works, which when recycled contributes to the evolution of crucial critical and historical studies and to catalogues raisonnés."[1]

Exhibition literature is a key information resource within art libraries. From private view cards, through free or cheap handlists and guides, to catalogues ranging from the ephemeral pamphlet to the substantial research publication, the visual and textual contents provide invaluable primary source material for the art researcher or scholar.

The importance and proliferation of such documentation makes more apparent the need for specialised guidance in dealing with these items. Although designed for use in the general library, the *Anglo-American Cataloguing Rules* 2nd ed. (AACR2)[2] remains the cataloguing code in common use within art libraries, providing rules for the consistent description of the individual item. Cataloguers dealing with exhibition documentation will know that many exhibition catalogues are ephemeral, displaying all the difficulties associated with grey literature. They frequently lack an orthodox "chief source of information", making it necessary to seek information from elsewhere in the document or from external sources. Important data elements may be missing and information such as the venue and dates of an exhibition, of significance in describing a catalogue but not bibliographic in character, may be difficult to place consistently within the structure of description established by the cataloguing code. Items may be published in a wide variety of physical formats, with exhibition catalogues in the form of posters, CD-ROMs or videocassettes commonly encountered.

The intrinsic difficulty presented by exhibition documentation is compounded by the fact that such items are governed by some of the more complex provisions of the cataloguing code. AACR2 rules governing choice of headings for a publication associated with a named event, for example in determining choice between corporate name (institution or event name) and personal name (artist or author) make this a particularly difficult area in which to apply the rules. Additional rules must be used when an exhibition catalogue is illustrated, and it is frequently necessary to make reference to a number of rules in conjunction and according to an agreed priority.

---

[1] Phillpot, Clive. *A cooperative project for retrospective conversion of cataloging records in four art museum libraries.* Application for funding from the Grant Program of the J. Paul Getty Trust, Jan.22, 1988, p.7

[2] *Anglo-American cataloguing rules.* 2nd ed., 1998 revision. Ottawa : Canadian Library Association ; London : Library Association ; Chicago : American Library Association, c1998.

Our intention here is to assist the cataloguer in making these choices. The guidelines are intended for the new cataloguer, the librarian working alone without the support of a cataloguing department, and the cataloguer working in a general library dealing with exhibition documentation on an occasional basis. In addition, it is hoped that the arguments presented here will be useful to those national agencies responsible for the collection and cataloguing of exhibition documentation by providing a framework for discussion.

1.1 History and development of the guidelines

The present publication has its origins in a document entitled *Problems of cataloguing exhibition catalogues: some guidelines,* drafted by the ARLIS UK & Ireland Cataloguing and Classification Committee in 1987. Although distributed widely within the art library community in the UK, these guidelines were never published. As a result of their development, a discussion document identifying areas of difficulty and proposing changes to AACR2 was submitted to the Library Association/British Library Committee responsible for considering and forwarding proposals for revision to the AACR2 Joint Steering Committee. In response, the LA/BL Committee suggested publication of the guidelines in an expanded form to supplement and explain the application of AACR2. In 1994, in a parallel development, the ARLIS UK & Ireland Committee for the National Co-ordination of Art Library Resources requested investigation of a minimum standard for cataloguing exhibition documentation. The present publication is an amalgamation of these two strands. The explanation of AACR2 rules and how to apply them has been expanded and an indication of a minimum standard included for each part of the catalogue record. Examples have been added throughout the text.

1.2 Relationship with AACR2

The present guidelines should be used in conjunction with AACR2 and the arrangement reflects this relationship. Guidance is provided for each area of the catalogue description, followed by explanation and clarification of the rules dealing with choice and form of headings. Although many of the relevant rules from AACR2 are discussed in detail below, there has been no attempt to reproduce aspects already fully and effectively covered by the main code; for example the detailed instructions covering the form of name headings are not reproduced here. Cataloguers implementing the guidelines must make reference to the main code as and where necessary and a concordance of rules is included to assist cross-referral. APPENDIX A contains certain key extracts from AACR2 and is intended to assist new cataloguers by picking out the information required to answer certain frequently asked questions. Where exhibition documentation presents particular difficulties, the guidelines supplement and expand upon the relevant AACR2 rule. For example, details of the hierarchy of rules used in determining main entry are discussed in Part II which deals with the choice and form of access points. This discussion is supplemented by a schematic representation of the rules in the flowchart at APPENDIX C.

AACR2 rules are arranged in a consistent order, reflecting the order of areas of the catalogue description set out in each chapter of AACR2. In the present guidelines

AACR2 rules may be quoted as, e.g. (AACR2 1.1, 2.1, etc.) to indicate that a parallel rule will be found in each subsequent chapter of AACR2 Part I, Description.

During the course of our work, much thought was given to presentation in a MARC based arrangement. The decision to retain an approach based upon the structure of AACR2 resulted from discussion of the draft guidelines at a cataloguing workshop in June 1998. At this workshop there was wide variation of experience with MARC in the art libraries represented, with some institutions using UKMARC, others USMARC and several of the smaller institutions making no use of MARC at all. UK and USMARC examples are included here at Part III.

1.3 Application of the guidelines: defining "exhibition documentation"

Libraries implementing the guidelines may choose to apply them to all publications relating to exhibitions; or they may opt to invoke a definition of an exhibition catalogue that excludes items published "on the occasion of " or "in conjunction with" an exhibition. In practice these categories are not easy to distinguish and implementation across all forms of documentation known to be associated with an exhibition may be preferable.

The connection with the exhibition may not be explicit on the title page but in many cases can be deduced from the connection with a museum or gallery and other evidence derived from prescribed sources as set out in the rules and/or from the content of the item.

The Glossary at AACR2 Appendix D gives one definition of a catalogue as:

```
"  ... a list of materials prepared for a particular purpose
(e.g., an exhibition catalogue ...)".
```

In the absence of an explicit statement that the item is a catalogue, the presence of a list of works in conjunction with dates and exhibition venue may indicate that an item is a catalogue. Other evidence suggesting a connection with an exhibition may be found on the title page verso, in the colophon, introduction and/or credits present on the item.

Look out for the following additional clues:

- Lists of venues
- Lists of institutions loaning works
- Lists of sponsors or patrons
- Introduction giving background to the organisation of the exhibition

To assist identification, relevant vocabulary in a range of European languages is included here at APPENDIX B.

In the absence of a list of works, the item may be regarded as a monograph "published on the occasion of the exhibition". Nonetheless it is strongly recommended that any link with an exhibition be recorded and accessible in the catalogue record as this may be critical for the user attempting to identify various publications associated with a particular exhibition or to distinguish between different publications with the same or very similar titles. It will also help library staff by alerting them to subsequent re-publication of a catalogue as a monograph.

Alongside the catalogues of temporary exhibitions, which include works drawn from a number of sources, a further category are those exhibitions comprising works derived from the permanent collection of a single institution. Such publications need to be distinguished from other temporary exhibitions if they are to be catalogued correctly according to AACR2 and they are covered in detail in the guidelines. Catalogues issued by dealers exhibiting work for sale also require slightly different treatment and are covered separately here.

1.4 The importance of exhibition documentation and national provision

In endeavouring to provide a path through the maze of relevant AACR2 rules, the intention is to improve consistency and ease of identification with the aim of promoting better access. At present, the ephemeral nature of many catalogues leads to poor coverage in the *British National Bibliography* as many catalogues slip through the legal deposit net. The benefits of co-operative initiatives such as the shared cataloguing of exhibition documentation established between the British Library and National Art Library will be assisted by greater consistency in cataloguing practice between the two institutions.

The moves to extend co-operation and standardisation through harmonisation of the MARC format and implementation by the Library of Congress, the British Library and their various partners of a single authority file, the Anglo-American Authority File (AAAF) provides welcome background to the work on exhibition documentation. The extension of cross-sector co-operation embodied in the foundation of MLAC is also relevant given its potential to extend the links between the producers of exhibition documentation with those making use of it. If the importance of exhibition documentation is appreciated and items effectively recorded, not only will we as librarians save ourselves time in locating these items, but also our library records will be of much greater value to the researcher.

INTRODUCTION

2. Constructing minimal level catalogue records (MLR): an introduction

The guidelines include notes on the construction of minimal level catalogue records (MLR) based upon AACR2 first level description. It is hoped that this approach will assist institutions lacking the resources to commit to full level cataloguing. Catalogue records constructed according to the MLR sections set out below will identify the item as a catalogue and provide schematic details of the exhibition to which it relates.

The following data elements constitute first level description, the level underpinning the minimal level record described here:

```
"Title    proper    /    first    statement    of    responsibility,    if
different   from   main   entry   heading   in   form   or   number   or   if
there   is   no   main   entry   heading.   -   Edition   statement.   -
Material   (or   type   of   publication)   specific   details.   -   First
publisher,   etc.,   date   of   publication,   etc.   -   Extent   of   item.   -
Note(s).   -   Standard   number."   -   (AACR2 1.0D1)
```

Cataloguers should include at least the above elements where applicable to the exhibition publication in hand. The rule permits the addition of further data elements as required by the cataloguing agency. The approach taken here has been to add further data elements to identify the relationship between the publication and event and/or to distinguish the specific catalogue from others with similar or identical titles.

Libraries choosing to implement this minimal or first level description may opt to apply this level of cataloguing to all items in a collection. Alternatively the library may choose to follow AACR2 0.29 by drawing up guidelines to determine when to make use of MLR cataloguing, for example in cataloguing exhibition publications of less than a certain size.

In applying first level description within a minimal level record, it should be noted that this does not restrict the number of subject headings added to the record. At this level, headings may be entered with less detailed justification within the descriptive entry. However some indication of the relationship between description and heading remains helpful for the catalogue user.

Instructions for minimal level record construction are set out in the sections marked MLR below. These sections are supplementary to the main text and should be read in conjunction with it. Where no MLR guidance is given, the cataloguer should follow the guidance given in the main text.

PART I

DESCRIPTION OF EXHIBITION DOCUMENTATION

3. Descriptive cataloguing

3.1 Chief source of information (AACR2 1.0A1, 2.0B1, etc.)

Before cataloguing can commence, a chief source of information to be used in constructing the catalogue description must be identified. The chief source provides the authoritative information to be used in describing the item. It is supplemented by other prescribed sources of information for each area of the description. Information taken from outside these prescribed sources is enclosed in square brackets by the cataloguer. In AACR2, each chapter of Part I covers a particular format or material type and includes details of the chief and prescribed sources to be used in cataloguing.

For items in printed form, AACR2 2.0B1 states:

```
"The chief source of information for printed monographs is the
title page..."
```

3.1.1 Items lacking a title page for use as the chief source of information

When dealing with exhibition catalogues, AACR2's emphasis upon the title page as chief source can cause difficulty. Exhibition catalogues are very diverse in format and appearance; standard bibliographic conventions may not be easy to apply. Items frequently lack a title page, or where present, the information given may be incomplete or presented over a number of successive or separated leaves as a graphic design device. The relationship between the publication and the exhibition may not be clearly stated on the title page or title page verso but may be revealed elsewhere in the item (preliminaries, introduction, colophon etc.) or from external sources (private view cards, press releases etc.).

In the absence of an identifiable title page, AACR2 2.0B1 provides guidance on what can be considered part of the title page or a substitute for it:

```
"The chief source of information for printed monographs is the
title page or, if there is no title page, the source from
within the publication that is used as a substitute for it. For
printed monographs published without a title page, or without a
title page applying to the whole work..., use the part of the
item supplying the most complete information, whether this be
the cover (excluding a separate book jacket), caption,
colophon, running title, or other part. Specify the part used
as a title page substitute in a note ... If no part of the item
supplies data that can be used as the basis of the description
take the necessary information from any available source. If
the information traditionally given on the title page is given
on facing pages or on pages on successive leaves, with or
without repetition, treat those pages as the title page. ..."
```

Thus, when an exhibition catalogue lacks a title page, the cataloguer should use AACR2 2.0B1 to decide on a substitute for it or, in the absence of any possible substitute, draw information from the content of the publication or from external sources such as press releases or private view cards. Information drawn from outside the selected chief source must be enclosed in square brackets.

3.1.2 Items with more than one title page

Items with more than one title page may also be encountered for example when two related exhibitions are issued back-to-back in a single publication.

Where an item includes more than one title page follow AACR2 1.0H1 in determining which to use as the chief source of information. This rule instructs that the first occurring chief source in a single item should generally be preferred. Among the exceptions given, the following have a particular relevance to the exhibition catalogue:

"a) In cataloguing an item comprising different works and with no chief source of information pertaining to the whole item, treat the sources of information for the different works as if they were a single source. Common examples include books containing a number of works with title pages for each..."

This will allow the cataloguer to combine the information contained in two separate title pages:

"d) For items that contain written ... words for which there are chief sources of information in more than one language or script, prefer, (in this order):

i) the source in the language or script of the written ... words if there is only one such language or script or only one predominant language or script

ii) the source in the original language or script of the work if the words are in more than one language or script..."

In determining the original language of the item, take note of the language of the originating body responsible for the exhibition.

"iii) the source in the language or script that occurs first in the following list : English, French, German, Spanish, Latin, any other language using the roman alphabet, Greek, Russian ... Hebrew, any other language..."

The above rules will assist the cataloguer dealing with the very many examples of catalogues with parallel title pages in different languages.

For exhibition catalogues in formats other than print, includes instruction on chief sources of information and their substitutes in the relevant chapters for non-print formats. See AACR2 6.0B (sound recordings), AACR2 7.0B (motion pictures and videorecordings), AACR2 8.0B (graphic materials), AACR2 9.0B (computer files).

3.2 Title and statement of responsibility area (AACR2 1.1, 2.1, etc.)

3.2.1 Title

The prescribed source of information for the title and statement of responsibility is the title page or its substitute (AACR2 2.0B2).

Note that hereafter in these guidelines, title page indicates the title page or any substitute selected as the chief source of information. Title page also refers by analogy to the chief sources used in cataloguing non-print formats.

The main title or "title proper" of the item should be transcribed exactly as it appears, following the wording, order and spelling but not necessarily the punctuation or capitalisation found in the chief source (AACR2 1.1B1). Capitalisation should follow the rules set out in APPENDIX A of AACR2 .[3]

Give the elements required in the title and statement of responsibility area in the order set out in AACR2 (AACR2 1.1, 2.1, etc.) even if this means transposing data appearing in the chief source (AACR2 1.1A2). Guidance on the transposition of artists' names appearing as part of the title is given below (See Section 3.2.2).

Where an item lacks any identifiable chief source of information a title should be supplied from the rest of the item or from a reference or other external source and the part used as a substitute indicated in a note. (AACR2 1.7B3, AACR2 2.7B3).

```
Title from cover

Title from private view card
```

Where no title can be identified, the cataloguer must devise a short descriptive title and enclose it in square brackets. In such circumstances record the fact in a note.

```
Title assigned by cataloguer
```

Occasionally there may be text at the head of title constituting neither title information nor a statement of responsibility. In the case of exhibition catalogues, statements relating to exhibition sponsorship are frequently encountered. Where such statements are not linked grammatically to the title they may be omitted (AACR2 1.1F15). If the cataloguing agency wishes to retain this information it may be given as a note.

---

[3]   "Title proper" is defined as "The chief name of an item, including any alternative title but excluding parallel titles and other title information." -- **AACR2 Glossary**.

```
At head of title: Sponsored by First National Bank
```

The title proper of the item may be followed by any "other title information" present in the chief source. This may take the form of a subtitle or may comprise a statement about the character or contents of the item, the motives for, or occasion of, its production or publication.[4]

If the statement that the item is a catalogue appears on the title page, include it as "other title information". If exhibition venues and dates appear on the title page, they should also be included. Where this information appears outside the chief source it should still be recorded but placed in the notes (see Section 3.7.1).

Where title proper or other title information is lengthy it may be abridged if this can be done "without loss of essential information" (AACR2 1.1B4, 1.1E3). However, it is recommended that other title information indicating the type of publication or its relationship to the exhibition be retained in the title area whenever possible, i.e. do not truncate information about the exhibition or transfer such information to the notes. Inclusion in the title area generally makes the information more accessible to the catalogue user.

In abridging a lengthy title proper or other title information, never omit the first five words. Indicate omissions using the mark of omission ". . .". (For additional guidance concerning inclusion or omission of artists' names appearing in titles see Section 3.2.2).

```
Tregaskis  Centenary  Exhibition  :  a  catalogue  of  the
Tregaskis  Centenary  Exhibition  1994,  ...  together with a
facsimile of the Tregaskis exhibition catalogue 1904 and
colour plates of the bindings in both exhibitions
```

> **MLR:** Lengthy titles may be abridged "without loss of essential information" (AACR2 1.1B4, 1.1E3). Where the title is truncated in this way, the first five words of the title should always be transcribed before the mark of omission ... (AACR2 1.1B4, 1.1E3). It is recommended that in MLR cataloguing the "title proper" should always be given in full to assist identification of the exhibition catalogue.

---

[4]   A definition of "other title information" is given in the Glossary to AACR2 and encompasses titles borne by the item other than title proper, parallel or series title.

Within AACR2 first level description, other title information may be omitted. However, it is recommended that subtitles appearing as part of other title information be retained where they clarify the subject coverage of the exhibition catalogue:

```
A common tradition : popular art of Britain and America ~:~
~exhibition catalogue, Brighton Festival, 6th - 24th May~
~1991~ ...
```

Section 3.2.2 and its associated MLR provide further examples for titles that include the artist's name.

Where exhibition details are present as "other title information" these details may be omitted from the title area if they are present in a concise form elsewhere in the record, for example where the venue is present as publisher:

```
Branwell Bronte and his circle : artistic life in
Bradford 1830-50 ~: a catalogue produced to accompany the~
~exhibition Branwell Bronte and his circle, artistic life~
~in Bradford 1830-50: 15 October 1994 - 29 January 1995,~
~Cartwright Hall, Bradford~ ...
Bradford : Cartwright Hall, 1994.
Catalogue of the exhibition held 1994-5.
```

A succinct "nature, scope or artistic form" note should always be added to identify the item as an exhibition catalogue where this information has been omitted from the title. The year of the exhibition may be extrapolated from the year of publication if they are one and the same. Where they differ add the year(s) of exhibition to the standard note (see Section 3.7 for further details concerning notes). In MLR cataloguing, an added entry for the venue or organising body may be made without explicit justification within the notes as long as the venue is present in either the title or the publication, distribution area.

Where the cataloguing agency prefers to retain further descriptive details of the exhibition in the title area, for example full dates, use the most concise form possible. The mark of omission should be used to indicate any intervening text that has been omitted:

```
Branwell Bronte and his circle: artistic life in Bradford
1830-50 ~: a catalogue produced to accompany the~
~exhibition Branwell Bronte and his circle, artistic life~
~in Bradford 1830-50~ ... : 15 October 1994 - 29 January
1995, Cartwright Hall, Bradford
```

3.2.2 Artists' names appearing as part of the title

In very many cases the cataloguer will need to decide how to treat the name(s) of artists appearing on the title page. The following rules offer guidance for some commonly encountered situations in which the artist's name could be interpreted as a statement of responsibility forming part of the title.

3.2.2.1 Artist's name appearing alone

"If the title proper consists solely of the name of a person or body responsible for the item, transcribe such a name as the title proper." -- AACR2 1.1B3

For many solo exhibitions the title proper is the artist's name and the name should be transcribed as the title proper, e.g.

    Henri Matisse

3.2.2.2 Artist's name followed by further title wording, which may or may not constitute "other title information"

The artist's name is frequently followed by a word or words indicating the type of exhibition or catalogue or the type of work included in the exhibition, e.g.

    Hockney's photographs

    Don McCullin : a retrospective

    Georges Braque : sculptures

    John Latham : early works, 1954-1972

    Bruce Nauman : exhibition catalogue and catalogue
    raisonné

According to AACR2 1.1B2:

"If the title proper includes a statement of responsibility ... and the statement ... is an integral part of the title proper (i.e., connected by a case ending or other grammatical construction), transcribe it as part of the title proper."

A complementary rule at AACR2 1.1F3 reads:

"If a statement of responsibility precedes the title proper in the chief source of information, transpose it to its required position unless it is an integral part of the title proper (see 1.1A2 and 1.1B20)".

The exhibition *Hockney's photographs* is an example of a title which is clearly covered by the first of these rules. There is no question of transposing the artist's name to follow the title as a statement of responsibility. Less clear cut are the other examples as these lack a grammatical link between artist's name and the remainder of the title. The artist is clearly the subject of the exhibition and yet can also be considered responsible for the intellectual and creative content of the works included in the catalogue. A solution may be found in AACR2 1.1B3 which instructs the cataloguer to transcribe a name appearing alone as title proper (see Section 3.2.2.1). Whenever the layout of the title page suggests that the remainder of the title is intended to be read as other title information, the cataloguer can invoke this rule and enter artist's name as title proper.

The more specific the title information following the name, the more difficult it is to determine whether to enter the artist's name as part of the title or as a statement of responsibility. The cataloguer must decide at which point the name ceases to be the "title proper" and requires transposition to form the statement of responsibility, a title such as:

    Stephen Willats : fateful combinations

could be entered as:

    Fateful combinations / Stephen Willats

In such cases the cataloguer should take account of the following in determining when to enter the artist's name as title proper:

a) Typographic layout
Is the name given prominence as title proper and the other wording as subtitle? If so enter the name as title proper.

    Bill Woodrow : Fools' gold
    (*Fools' gold is the title of a work by the artist*)

    Joseph Beuys : the revolution is us

    Clovio : miniaturist of the Renaissance

b) Is another individual named in the chief source as having primary responsibility for the item?
If so retain the artist's name as title proper.

    Mondrian : nature to abstraction : from the
    Gemeentemuseum, The Hague / Bridget Riley

c) Is the named artist likely to have a responsibility extending beyond that of creator of works in the exhibition?
If so and the criteria in a) and b) do not apply, transpose the name to the statement of responsibility position.

```
Archiving my own history : documentation of works 1969 >
1994 / Rose Garrard
```

In the example above the artist is credited with responsibility for research and collation and provides extensive text.

It is not necessary to include the artist's name in a statement of responsibility in order to justify artist "main entry" i.e. to support a decision to assign primary intellectual responsibility for the item to the artist (see Section 6.5.2).

In case of doubt retain the name as part of title.

3.2.2.3 Artist's name follows the title proper

Where the name of the artist follows the title proper and is itself followed by other title information retain it as part of the title:

```
Hot air : Jonathan Allen, Mappin Art Gallery, Sheffield,
24th April-6th June 1993
```

Where the name of the artist follows the title proper and there is no other title information, the name may be a candidate for treatment as a statement of responsibility. In such cases look out for the following:

a) Typography and the wording of the title
If the artist's name appears as part of the title wherever the item is described, e.g. in running title, publisher's description etc. retain this as part of the title. Look out for elements emphasising a reading of the artist's role as subject of the catalogue, for example the presence of dates following the name.

b) Is another individual named in the chief source as having primary responsibility for the item?
If so retain the artist's name as part of the title proper.

```
Early works : Lucian Freud / Richard Calvocoressi
```

```
Sacred & profane : Calum Colvin / [by] James Lawson
```

c) Is the named artist likely to have a responsibility extending beyond that of creator of works in the exhibition?
If so and the criteria in a) and b) do not apply, the name should be regarded as a statement of responsibility.

Once again it should be stressed that the decision to place the artist's name in the title area does not rule out choice of the artist's name as main entry, i.e. regarding the artist as the person bearing primary responsibility for the intellectual or artistic content of the item. In case of doubt retain the artist's name as part of the title.

3.2.2.4 Artists' names present in the title: treatment in the statement of responsibility area

Where the name of an individual is included in the title do not repeat it as a statement of responsibility (AACR2 1.1F13).

> **MLR**: In applying the rules set out in the preceding sections, those agencies cataloguing at MLR level should ensure that various catalogues entered under the artist's name as title proper can be distinguished. Retain any subtitle or other title information necessary to achieve this. Where the name of an artist appears as part of a subtitle, it should be retained as it clarifies the subject of the catalogue (see Section 3.2.4 and the associated MLR).

3.2.2.5 Lists of artists' names appearing as part of the title

Where several artists are listed on the title page, whether these constitute title proper or other title information, the mark of omission may be used to abbreviate the list where lengthy. Since AACR2 1.1B4 and AACR2 1.1E3 state that the first five words of the title should always be included, sufficient names must be transcribed to fulfil this requirement. It is recommended that the names of up to three artists should in any case always be included where these appear in the title proper or as other title information. Where more than three names are present, it is recommended that the first three should still be given to assist identification of the relevant catalogue. More may be given at the discretion of the cataloguing agency.[5] Where the names are listed as other title information, the same recommendation to list the first three applies. Where the mark of omission is used, do not use the convention [et al.]. Confine this usage to the statement of responsibility.

If certain of the artists' names, which would not normally be transcribed, are of particular significance to the cataloguing agency, record them in a note (see Section 3.7.6).

```
Kent, Sarah
Young British artists : John Greenwood, Damien Hirst,
Alex Landrum ... / text by Sarah Kent
```

---

[5]   National Art Library policy is to transcribe up to six names. Tate Gallery Library policy is to include up to ten, giving preference to artists little documented, those well documented in the catalogue to hand and British artists.

Exhibited artists include: Rachel Whiteread

MLR: Include at least the first three names in any title proper. Where a list of artists' names is present in the chief source as other title information this may be omitted. Headings for relevant names may still be made as required by the cataloguing agency.

3.2.3 General material designation (GMD) (AACR2 1.1C)

Alongside printed publications, exhibition catalogues appear in many other formats; from the acoustiguide catalogue on cassette to the catalogue mounted on the Internet.

Where records are to be held together in a single library catalogue, the addition of a general material designator [GMD] is recommended. This optional element is a term indicating the material/format of the publication. For exhibition publications appearing in non-book formats, give the GMD in square brackets after the title proper:[6]

> Making Aalto's furniture [videorecording] / produced, written and narrated by J. Stewart Johnson

> Drawn to seeing [computer file] : works in pencil on paper / by Michael Heindorff

For exhibition catalogues in electronic form use the GMD [computer file], or where appropriate [interactive multimedia].[7] Where an electronic format is catalogued supplement the GMD with an appropriate "file characteristic" from the list set out in *ISBD(ER): International Standard Bibliographic Description for Electronic Resources, revised from the ISBD(CF), International Standard Bibliographic Description for Computer Files*, as recommended by the ISBD(CF) Review Group.[8]

For the full list of GMD terms available for use see the list at AACR2 1.1C1.

MLR: Although the GMD may be omitted in MLR cataloguing, its inclusion is recommended where exhibition documentation is collected in all formats for inclusion in a single catalogue. This will assist the identification of the appropriate format by the catalogue end-user.

---

[6]   AACR includes two lists of General Material Designations to be used in cataloguing. List 1 applies to British Agencies (applicable to most UK libraries using UKMARC); list 2 applies to cataloguing agencies in the US, Australia and Canada (and is also used by UK libraries using USMARC).

[7]   AACR2 use of the GMD computer file is likely to be replaced by the term electronic resource as part of ongoing revision of AACR2.

[8]   ISBD(ER) : International Standard Bibliographic Description for Electronic Resources, revised from the ISBD(CF), International Standard Bibliographic Description / recommended by the ISBD(CF) Review Group. München : Saur, 1997. ISBN 3598113692.

3.2.4 Other titles (collective, alternative, parallel, variant)

Exhibition catalogues frequently present multiple titles. A single publication may contain the catalogue of a second or subsequent exhibition with its own title page. The title of a catalogue may be given in various forms or in more than one language on a single chief source of information or on a separate title page. The following rules are intended to assist the cataloguer in distinguishing between types of title encountered and to show how each one can be dealt with under the provisions of AACR2.

3.2.4.1 Collective titles (AACR2 1.1B10)

"A title proper that is an inclusive title for an item containing several works".[9]

If the chief source of information for an item bears a collective title and the titles of the individual contained works, give the collective title as the title proper. Give the titles of individual works in a contents note (AACR2 1.1B10).

```
Electronic undercurrents.
[Copenhagen] : Statens Museum for kunst, c1996-
Published on the occasion of the exhibition with the same
title held at the Statens Museum for kunst, Sept. 7-Nov.
30, 1996.
Contents: Art & video in Europe / Lars Movin & Torben
Christensen -- American film & video : Whitney Biennial /
[organisation of exhibition and catalogue, Vibeke
Petersen and Marianne Torp Øckenholt] -- Video sculptures
/ Nam June Paik
```

In the above example the catalogue contains a number of individual bibliographic works. Name/title added entries may be made as required by the cataloguing agency.

3.2.4.2 Items lacking a collective title (AACR2 1.1G1-1.1G4)

Where an item has no collective title but contains more than one bibliographic work, for example a publication containing more than one exhibition catalogue in a single volume, give the title of the predominant work as title proper, and the second or subsequent titles in a contents note. Where no one work predominates, transcribe the titles in the order in which they appear in the chief source of information, or if the publication has no single chief source of information, transcribe them in the order in which they appear in the item, treating the multiple chief sources as a single source (AACR2 1.0H1 a)).

```
Fougstedt, Arvid
Arvid Fougstedt.  Erik Wessel-Fougstedt
```

---

[9] AACR2 Appendix D. Glossary. Note that "works" in this context means individually titled bibliographic works and not the works contained within the exhibition.

In the above example, there is no collective title and the works are issued tête-bêche (or back-to-back). The two title pages have therefore been treated as a single chief source of information and both titles given as if from a single source. The second title can be given an added title entry and the second named artist an added name heading.

3.2.4.3 Alternative titles (AACR2 1.1B1, 2.1B1, etc.)

Alternative titles are encountered when an item bears two proper titles linked by the word 'or' (or its equivalent in another language). Both titles are included in the title proper. Precede and follow the word introducing the alternative title with commas. Capitalise the first word of the alternative title. The alternative title should be given an added title entry point (see Section 7.2.8).

```
Landscape, or, Nature and art
The catalogue of an exhibition held at the DLI Museum and
Arts Centre, 1974
```

Make an added title entry for the alternative title:

```
Nature and art
```

3.2.4.4 Parallel Titles (AACR2 1.1D, 2.1D, etc.)

Parallel titles are often encountered in multilingual catalogues associated with touring exhibitions. Transcribe parallel titles in the order indicated by their sequence on, or by the layout of, the chief source of information (AACR2 1.1D1).

Occasionally, parallel titles appear on the title page of a work containing text in only one language. If the work is not a translation of a previously published work, then the titles are still transcribed as parallel titles. If the work is a translation, the original title is only recorded as a parallel title if it appears before the title proper, or if the item contains some of the text in the original language (AACR2 1.1D3).

If parallel titles appear on different chief sources, for example at opposite ends of the item, the primary source of information must be identified, following AACR2 1.0H1(d). The second or subsequent title appearing on the second (added) title page should be recorded in a note supplemented by an added title entry.

```
Gevurot le-Ayalah : Omamut Yi re elit me-osfe Ayalah Zaks
Abramov
Title on added t.p.: A tribute to Ayala
```

Make an added title entry for:

```
Tribute to Ayala
```

If there are a number of parallel subtitles following the title proper, and the title proper appears in only one language, transcribe only the subtitle in the language of the title proper; if this criterion does not apply, transcribe the first one which appears (AACR2 1.1E5).

If a parallel title appears elsewhere in the item (i.e. outside the chosen chief source of information), record it in a note (AACR2 1.1D4, 1.7B5).

Make added title entries where these provide useful additional access points (see Section 7.2.8).

Note that where a statement of responsibility appears in association with one or more parallel titles but is present in one language only, it should be placed at the end of the sequence of parallel titles and subtitles.

MLR: Parallel titles are not usually transcribed at this level, although an added title heading may be made at the discretion of the cataloguing agency. It is recommended that a parallel title should be included where the main title is in a language other than English and an English parallel title is present on the item. In addition make an added title entry for the parallel title in English.

```
Meister  der  Einbandkunst  =  Masters  of  the  art  of
bookbinding  = Maîtres de la reliure d'art
Masters of the art of bookbinding
```

Parallel other title information should be omitted.

```
Allen Jones, 1957-1978: retrospective of paintings: an
exhibition = Gemalde: eine Au tellung / organised by the
Walker Art Gallery, Liverpool; text by Marco Livingstone
```

3.2.4.5 Variant titles (AACR2 1.7B4, 2.7B4, etc.)

When dealing with variations in the title appearing on the item, for example where the title given on the spine or cover differs from the title as presented in the chief source, details should be given in the notes, e.g.

```
Tina Gloriani : European touring exhibition of sculpture
and painting
```

This includes the following variant spine title, which should be given in a note:

```
Spine title: Light and shadow in forms
```

An added title entry may be made for any title likely to be sought by the catalogue user (see Section 7.2.8).

3.2.5 Statements of responsibility (AACR2 1.1F, 2.1F, etc.)

The statement of responsibility is defined in the AACR2 Glossary as:

"A statement, transcribed from the item being described, relating to persons responsible for the intellectual or artistic content of the item, to corporate bodies from which the content emanates, or to persons or corporate bodies responsible for the performance of the content of the item."

In printed exhibition documentation, the title page is the prescribed source for the statement of responsibility (AACR2 2.0B2) and the statement should be transcribed exactly as it appears there:

"Transcribe statements of responsibility appearing prominently in the item in the form in which they appear there. If a statement of responsibility is taken from a source other than the chief source of information, enclose it in square brackets." -- AACR2 1.1F1

Thus names appearing outside the prescribed source but prominently within the item (i.e. outside the title page but present in the title page verso, preliminaries or colophon) should be included in the title area, enclosed in square brackets.[10]

If no statement of responsibility appears prominently in the item, and the cataloguer identifies one from elsewhere in the item or from external sources, it should not be included in the title area. Instead, give the relevant information in a note. (AACR2 1.1F2, 1.7B6).

Each statement of responsibility may include the names of up to three persons or corporate bodies. Where more than three persons or bodies performing the same function are named in a single statement of responsibility, follow AACR2 1.1F5 in giving the first named only, followed by the mark of omission . . . [et al.]

Exhibition catalogues frequently include multiple statements of responsibility associated with both the publication and the event and these must be carefully disentangled. Take particular care in transcribing multiple statements appearing on the item to ensure that these statements are given unambiguously. Make use of the rule at AACR2 1.1F6:

---

[10] "The word *prominently* (used in such phrases as prominently named and stated prominently) means that a statement to which it applies must be a formal statement found in one of the prescribed sources of information for areas 1 and 2 for the class of material to which the item being catalogued belongs". (AACR2 0.8) For a printed book this includes title page or titlepage verso, any pages preceding the title page, the cover and colophon (see also APPENDIX A).

"... transcribe ... in the order indicated by their sequence on, or the layout of, the chief source of information. If the sequence and layout are ambiguous or insufficient to determine the order, transcribe the statements in the order that makes the most sense. If statements of responsibility appear in sources other than the chief source, transcribe them in the order that makes the most sense."   (AACR2 1.1F6)

Follow AACR2 1.1F15 in omitting statements that do not constitute either other title information or responsibility for intellectual or artistic content. Thus statements relating to the physical production of the work or the exhibition, naming designers or production editors, or those concerned with exhibition sponsorship should not be recorded in the statement of responsibility area although they may be given in the notes as required by the cataloguing agency.

When dealing with exhibition documentation, the person named in the statement of responsibility may be the curator responsible for an exhibition, while the exhibition catalogue may represent the collective contribution of various individuals and organisations. Where this is the case, insert a short phrase to explain the relationship between the item and the person(s) or body (bodies) named on the title page (AACR2 1.1F8, 2.1F2). Use wording such as:

        [exhibition organised by]

        [catalogue editor]

        [exhibition curated by]

Such terms may be appropriate even where the named individual is responsible for the only significant text in the item, if a number of other individuals are credited elsewhere, for example on the title page verso.

In other circumstances such a phrase may be needed to indicate the extent of the contribution.

        [introduction by]

        [catalogue entries compiled by]

Instructions for dealing with artists' names appearing as part of the title within the statement of responsibility area are given at Section 3.2.2 above).

Follow AACR2 1.1F14 and include statements of responsibility appearing in the item even where they do not name an individual or body.

MLR: Follow AACR2 1.0D1 first level description and include the first statement of responsibility only where this differs from the main entry heading for the item in form or number or if there is no main entry heading:

```
Rogerson, Ian
Noel Carrington and his Puffin picture books : an
exhibition catalogue / Ian Rogerson

Snowdon, Antony Armstrong-Jones, Earl of, 1930-
Serendipity / by Snowdon
```

In other words, where a single author/artist is considered to have responsibility and is accorded main entry, the statement of responsibility can be excluded, provided it is entered in the same form as the access point. Where it is different, retain the statement.

If the only difference is the presence of dates following the name in the heading consider the statement and heading to be identical in form and omit the statement.

A single statement of responsibility naming more than one person or body will be included because it differs from the main entry heading in number:

```
Johnstone, Stephen
The alien and the domestic : Laura Godfrey-Isaacs / text
by Stephen Johnstone with Laura Godfrey-Isaacs, Leah
Kharibian and Jon Graystone
Godfrey-Isaacs, Laura
```

Refer to Section 3.2.2.2 to determine when to transpose the name of an artist appearing as part of the title to the statement of responsibility area. In MLR cataloguing, applying AACR2 1.1F3 to transpose the artist's name to follow the title may mean that the name is omitted following the rules given here.

Omit any second or subsequent statements of responsibility unless inclusion is recommended by the following rules.

In MLR cataloguing, names appearing outside the chief source of information but within the prescribed sources are less likely to be included in the statement of responsibility area. Where exceptions are encountered, the name should be given in square brackets. If required by the cataloguing agency, names appearing outside the title page verso, preliminaries and colophon, i.e. non-prominently may be given in the notes (AACR2 1.1F2). As indicated in the main text above, a short phrase indicating, for example, [accompanying text by], or [catalogue editor] etc. may be inserted (AACR2 1.1F8, 2.1F2) to explain the nature of responsibility.

3.3 Edition area (AACR2 1.2, 2.2, etc.)

AACR2 2.2B1 instructs the cataloguer to:

"Transcribe a statement relating to an edition of a work that contains differences from other editions of that work, or to a named reissue of that work..."

In cataloguing exhibition catalogues, edition statements are relatively infrequent but where present they should be transcribed.

```
St Ives 1939-64 : twenty five years of painting, sculpture
and pottery. - Rev. ed.
Originally published: London : Tate Gallery, 1985. -
Contains a substantially updated chronology and list of
exhibitions
```

Much more commonly encountered are variant editions lacking a formal edition statement. These are often published to accompany the exhibition as it moves from venue to venue. They range from the parallel edition with a different title page, ISBN and imprint through to examples which have the same imprint and ISBN and appear identical in every way until close examination reveals slight variations in the works or the illustrations included.

An optional rule in AACR2 allows the cataloguer to supply an edition statement where an item is known to have changed significantly:

"If an item lacks an edition statement but is known to contain significant changes from other editions, supply a suitable brief statement in the language and script of the title proper and enclose it in square brackets" - (AACR2 2.2B3)

However, it is recognised that cataloguers will rarely have the resources to make the detailed comparisons necessary in determining the extent of differences between parallel editions. It is recommended that this optional rule should NOT be used to deal with parallel editions of this type. Instead the cataloguer should make full use of the publication, distribution area in combination with the statement of extent to bring out any publication and physical differences between the variants. A note indicating the presence of a parallel publication should be included where this information is available. In the vast majority of cases this should be sufficient to highlight the presence of a parallel edition. Compare the following examples:

```
Rhie, Marylin M.
The sacred art of Tibet : wisdom and compassion / Marylin
M. Rhie, Robert A. F. Thurman ; photographs by John
Bigelow Taylor
London : Thames and Hudson, 1991
Catalogue of the exhibition "Wisdom and compassion: the
sacred art of Tibet" organized by the Asian Art Museum of
San Francisco with Tibet House, New York City, in 1991
Rhie, Marylin M.
```

```
The sacred art of Tibet : wisdom and compassion / Marylin
M. Rhie, Robert A.F. Thurman ; photographs by John Bigelow
Taylor
Special reprint ed.
London : Royal Academy of Arts ; New York : In association
with H.N. Abrams, Inc., 1992, c1991
Catalogue of the exhibition organized by the Asian Art
Museum of San Francisco with Tibet House, New York City,
and held at the Asian Art Museum of San Francisco, 17
April-18 Aug. 1991, IBM Gallery of Science and Art, New
York City, 15 Oct.-28 Dec. 1991, Royal Academy of Arts,
London, 18 Sept.-13 Dec. 1992
```

Where the author or title of the edition in hand differs from that of a previous edition, this information should be given in a note, with an author-title or title added entry.

```
London in paint : oil paintings in the collection at the
Museum of London
Rev. and expanded ed. / Mireille Galinou and John Hayes.
Previous ed. published as : Catalogue of oil paintings in
the London Museum / John Hayes
```

The treatment of statements of responsibility relating to the edition area is covered by AACR2 1.2C, 2.2C, etc.

> **MLR:** Always include the edition statement where applicable. Where parallel editions are encountered, give concise information concerning the parallel edition in the notes when this can be readily ascertained.

3.4 Publication, distribution, etc., area (AACR2 1.4, 2.4, etc.)

3.4.1 Place of publication (AACR2 1.4C, 2.4C, etc.)

AACR2 instructs that place of publication should be transcribed in the form and the grammatical case in which it appears on the item, e.g. Firenze. For detailed instructions see AACR2 1.4C.

Where two or more places associated with a single publisher are named, give the first name. Add any second or subsequent name associated with the name of an exhibition organiser or venue cited as publisher given prominence by layout or typography. If the first named place is not in the country of the cataloguing agency add the first of any subsequently named place that is. (AACR2 1.4C5).

3.4.2 Publisher, distributor (AACR2 1.4D, 2.4D, etc.)

Give the name of the publisher, distributor following the place name to which it relates in the shortest form in which it can be understood or identified internationally (AACR2 1.4D2).

```
London : National Portrait Gallery ; New York : Dover
Publications, 1995
```

If the publisher is a gallery or museum whose name appears in a recognizable form in the title or statement of responsibility area, AACR2 1.4D4 prescribes using "the shortest possible form" such as The Gallery.

```
Royal Hibernian Academy (Dublin, Ireland)
A selection from the UTV collection of paintings : an
exhibition at the Royal Hibernian Academy, Dublin, 25
Mar.- 4 Apr. 1993. - Dublin : The Academy, 1993
```

Note that exhibition catalogues are frequently and increasingly joint publications reflecting shared responsibility for the exhibition as a result of joint sponsorship or publishing ventures. AACR2 instructs that an item with two or more publishers should be described in terms of the first named publisher and the corresponding place(s) (AACR2 1.4D5). However, this AACR2 rule gives various exceptions, the following having a particular relevance to the cataloguing of exhibition catalogues:

```
"a) when the first and subsequently named entities are linked
in a single statement"
```

Exhibition catalogues issued jointly by the host organisation and a commercial publisher frequently express this in the publication statement. Where more than one organisation is responsible for organising and hosting the exhibition this is also frequently reflected by shared responsibility for the publication:

```
Hudson Hills Press in association with the Yale Center
for British Art

Yale University Press in association with Leeds City Art
Galleries and the Victoria and Albert Museum

Robert Mann Gallery in conjunction with the Simon Neuman
Gallery
```

```
"c) when a subsequently named entity is clearly distinguished
as the principal publisher, distributor etc., by layout or
typography"
```

Where the exhibition organiser and/or an exhibition venue is assigned responsibility in the imprint as publisher, the dual role provides sufficient additional emphasis to warrant inclusion in the publication, distribution area even where the body is not named first.

```
    New York : Abrams ; Phoenix : Phoenix Art Museum
```

"d) when the subsequently named publisher, distributor, etc. is in the home country of the cataloguing agency and the first named publisher, distributor, etc. is not."

```
    Munich : Prestel ; London : Royal Academy of Arts, 1993
```

This is for an exhibition publication catalogued by an agency in the UK.

Exhibition catalogues self-published by the artist are fairly frequently encountered. In such cases give the initials and surname of the artist following AACR2 1.4D4 or enter as The Artist. Where no publisher can be identified enter as [s.n.].

3.4.3 Date of publication (AACR2 1.4F, 2.4F, etc.)

"For published items, give the date (i.e., year) of publication, distribution etc. of the edition, revision etc. named in the edition area. If there is no edition statement, give the date of the first publication of the edition to which the item belongs." (AACR2 1.4F1).

AACR2 1.4F1 provides full instructions concerning the entry of date of publication.
In the absence of a date of publication, follow AACR2 1.4F7 and supply a date using the evidence of the dates of exhibition. Record the date in square brackets if it is inferred from the exhibition dates.

MLR: The publication details to be included are:

Place of publication
Although AACR2 First level description provides for the omission of the place of publication, its inclusion is recommended at this level as this may assist the identification of place of exhibition where information given elsewhere in the record is very concise. Where place of publication is included, give the first place only.
A subsequent place in the country of the cataloguing agency may usefully be added if the exhibition was held there.

Publisher, distributor, etc
First publisher only, unless there is a statement linking two publishers or a publisher and a corporate body, in which case record the full details (AACR2 1.4D5a). Follow the main text above in giving the shortest form of publisher's name. Include any subsequently named British publisher.

Date
Record as instructed in AACR2.

3.5 Physical description area (AACR2 1.5, 2.5, etc.)

Exhibition catalogues vary enormously in their physical form and the inclusion of a statement of physical extent may be the most effective means to distinguish the short exhibition guide from the full catalogue where other elements are identical.

Catalogues are often physically ephemeral and frequently contain unnumbered sequences of pages and plates. Illustration statements may also be complex (see AACR2 2.5B, 2.5C). Physical format may also be unusual in the sequence or shape or size of pages. Make full use of descriptive notes to supplement the physical description area.

Catalogues may be published in a range of other formats and the relevant chapters of AACR2 should be used to determine the appropriate physical description for items published as audio or videocassettes, on CD-ROM etc. The notes that follow deal in the main with printed catalogues.

3.5.1 Extent

Follow AACR2 1.5 and relevant sections in the subsequent chapters of AACR2 Part I. Description in establishing the extent of item. For printed items, this statement of extent should include the following where appropriate:

The number of physical items, where more than one, e.g.

        2 v.

Number of pages or leaves in a single item, e.g.

        25 p.

Note that unnumbered sequences counted by the cataloguer are given in square brackets.

        [35] p.

whereas if the number is estimated it should be given without square brackets preceded by ca.

        ca. 250 p.

AACR2 instructs that unnumbered sequences of advertising material should be disregarded in determining pagination.

Where sequences of plates are present in the item, these should be given following the sequences of pagination whether found together or distributed throughout the item, e.g.

```
25 p., [12] leaves of plates
```

Describe folded leaves as such following AACR2 2.5B11.

When an item contains two separate catalogues paginated back to back, follow AACR2 2.5B15 in giving the pagination in sequence, starting with the physical description of the item given first in the title area.

Where pages are unnumbered and too numerous to count, the extent may be given as:

```
1 v.
```

In distinguishing ephemeral items from large unpaginated volumes make use of the alternative terms suggested by AACR2 2.5B18. Thus if the cataloguer does not count or estimate the number of pages, select the most appropriate term from the list to give a more precise indication of the physical form of the item, e.g.

```
1 pamphlet
1 portfolio
1 case
```

For catalogues in other formats, the relevant chapters of AACR2 give suitable terms:

```
1 poster
1 computer optical disc
1 sound cassette (ca. 30 min.)
```

3.5.2 Illustration statement (AACR2 2.5C)

For printed catalogues, follow the guidance in AACR2 2.5C and indicate that the item is illustrated. Note the instruction at AACR2 2.5C5 to indicate `chiefly ill., all ill.` as appropriate and combine this with an indication of the presence of colour illustrations where necessary (AACR2 2.5C3).

```
258 p. : ill. (some col.)

56 p. : chiefly col. ill.
```

Where the illustrations are all of one or more of the types given in the list at AACR2 2.5C2 use the appropriate term or abbreviation e.g.

```
30 p. : ports.

92 p. : chiefly coats of arms
```

Follow AACR2 2.5C2 in giving `ill.` first if only some of the illustrations are of one of the listed types, e.g.

```
50 p. : ill (some col.), facsims.
```

3.5.3 Dimensions (AACR2 1.5D, 2.5D etc.)

Enter as instructed in AACR2 1.5D and in subsequent chapters. For printed catalogues give the height in cm. to the next whole cm. (AACR2 2.5D1).

Note that exhibition catalogues published in the form of posters require the recording of the unfolded and folded dimensions (AACR2 2.5D4):

```
1 poster : col. ; 48 x 30 cm. folded to 24 x 15 cm.
```

3.5.4 Accompanying material (AACR2 1.5E, 2.5E etc.)

Give the details of accompanying material as instructed in AACR2 1.5E and subsequent chapters. Note that exhibition catalogues may often be accompanied by a list of works issued as a separate leaf and in some cases by a private view card. In other cases significant accompanying material such as folded posters, postcards or transparencies may be present. Record these at the end of the physical description field.

Where a separate duplicated list of works and/or a private view card accompanies the published catalogue, the cataloguing agency may choose to keep these items with the catalogue. If this is the case, record them as accompanying material and add further description in the notes if required.

```
32 p. : ill. (some col.), port. ; 24 cm. + 1 private view
card ([4] p. : ill. ; 15 cm.)
```

MLR: (See also AACR2 1.5 and the relevant sections of subsequent chapters). The elements of physical description to be included are:

Extent

Give the number of physical items and pagination or equivalent where the item is paginated, e.g.

```
1 v.
25 p.
```

In MLR cataloguing it is recognised that many institutions may prefer not to count pages and plate sequences in unpaginated items. As a minimum, it is recommended that the cataloguer records the extent of all paginated items but where no page numbers are present physical extent should be expressed using the convention 1 v. to indicate a single item. Select an appropriate alternative term from the list at AACR2 2.5B18 to indicate those items that are particularly ephemeral, e.g.

```
1 pamphlet
1 folded leaf
1 portfolio
```

Record separate sequences of plates appearing in paginated items as instructed in the main text above:

```
    12 leaves of plates
```

Illustration statement

In recording the illustration statement do not include details of specific types of illustration unless all or most of the illustrations belong to the specific type. Thus,
```
    ports.
    chiefly ill., ~~ports~~
```

Dimensions

Record as indicated in the main text above.

Accompanying material

Significant accompanying material may be recorded at the end of the physical description field. A simple statement of form is sufficient at this level, e.g.

```
    + 1 poster
```

3.6 Series area (AACR2 1.6, 2.6, etc.)

The series statement should be recorded as instructed in AACR2 1.6, 2.6.

```
    Art from Britain ; v. 2
    Studies in Asian art ; no. 3
    Spotlight (South Bank Centre)
```

MLR: Omit series statements, in accordance with AACR2 1.0D1.

3.7 Note area (AACR2 1.7, 2.7, etc.)

Make all the notes described below where applicable to the item. Notes contain useful additional information that cannot be fitted into other areas of the description. An outline of the various types of note is given at AACR2 1.7B and in subsequent chapters. The comments below are intended to highlight issues associated with exhibition-related documentation only. Where appropriate, notes should be combined as indicated by AACR2 1.7A5 to provide additional information in the most helpful and succinct form.

MLR: Notes should be kept to a minimum. It is recommended that the **Nature, scope, or artistic form** note is included to indicate that an item is a catalogue and that the **Edition** and **Publication history** notes is used to indicate the relationship to the exhibition (see Sections 3.7.1, 3.7.7, 3.7.8 below). In a minimal level record, it is not necessary to justify all the information conveyed in access points within the notes.

3.7.1 Nature, scope, or artistic form (AACR2 1.7B1, 2.7B1, etc.)

When the information that an item is a catalogue is not given in the title and statement of responsibility area, include this in a note.

```
Exhibition catalogue
```

Where the catalogue is in a language other than English and all essential data relating to the exhibition is present in the title field, still include the words "Exhibition catalogue" in the notes.

Where identifying details of the exhibition are not present in the title area, use a standard form of note to provide information about the item and the exhibition to which it relates. Give the venue, place and year wherever possible.

```
Catalogue of the exhibition held at the Museum of Modern
Art, New York, 10 Oct. - 24 Nov. 1996
```

If the publication relates to a touring exhibition, give the names of up to three venues. If more than three are known to be responsible, name only the first venue unless a subsequent venue is of particular importance to the cataloguing agency, e.g. a subsequent venue is based in the same country as the cataloguing agency. When venues are too numerous to list, indicate that the exhibition toured by the words "and travelling". Give the dates associated with the opening venue and a closing date for the tour if possible.

```
Catalogue of an exhibition held at San Francisco Museum
of Modern Art, 19 Dec. 1991 - 15 Mar. 1992 and travelling
throughout the USA until 27 Mar. 1994
```

Notes can also be used to support and explain the presence of an added entry for the name of the exhibition (where this differs from the title given in the title area) (see Section 7.2.6).

```
"Updated guide published as a companion to the catalogue
of the exhibition A Gift to the Nation: the Fine and
Decorative Art Collections of Ernest E. Cook, held at the
Holburne Museum and Crafts Study Centre, Bath, 16 May - 1
Sept. 1991" - T.p. verso
```

In some cases it may be easier to quote from the item and give the source of the information, rather than for the cataloguer to compose the note. AACR2 1.7A2 and AACR2 1.7A3 provide guidance on quoting from the item; the source of information quoted should always be given unless the information comes from the title page.

If the item is described as, or known to be, a book published on the occasion of an exhibition, and this is not explicitly stated in the title area, include this information here. Give it in a standard form, or quote from the item if possible:

```
Published to accompany the exhibition held at the Royal
Academy, London, 1 Oct.- 20 Dec. 1996
```

MLR: Follow the above guidelines but keep notes to a minimum. Given that the description is abbreviated and the nature of the publication may not be apparent, include the note "Exhibition catalogue", or, "Published on the occasion of the exhibition ..." as appropriate where this information is not given in the title and statement of responsibility area.

Full dates of the exhibition may be given at the discretion of the cataloguing agency. Give exact dates where these can be identified from the item. As a minimum the year of exhibition should be included in the catalogue record. Give this in the notes where it is not present in the title or the publication, distribution area. Where the year of exhibition is identical to the date of publication, there is no need to repeat it in the notes. The juxtaposition of venue and date within the publication, distribution area combined with the statement that the item is an exhibition catalogue should serve to identify the relationship with the exhibition.

Information included in the title proper should not be repeated in the notes.

Indicate that the catalogue relates to a travelling exhibition by including this information in a concise form.

```
Catalogue of an exhibition held San Francisco Museum of
Modern Art, 19 Dec. 1991 - 15 Mar. 1992 and travelling
throughout the USA until 27 Mar. 1994
```

If the details of the opening venue and dates have already been given in the title or publication, distribution area, there is no need to repeat them in the notes:

```
Catalogue of the exhibition travelling until 1994
```

3.7.2 Language of the item and/or translation or adaptation (AACR2 1.7B2, 2.7B2, etc.)

Use this note to record information about the language of an item where this is not apparent from the title area. If an item is a translation, or if it contains parallel text in two or more languages, or has a summary in a language other than the main language of the item, give details in a note, e.g.

```
Italian text, parallel English translation
```

Include a note to indicate the presence of captions or a summary in English where the bulk of the text is in another language.

Where the catalogue is in a language other than English and information about the exhibition is not present in the title area, give this information in the notes. Prefer to give such a note in English to assist catalogue users rather than quoting in the language of the item.

Where the title of the item is the artist's name always include a note about the language if this is other than English.

3.7.3 Source of title proper (AACR2 1.7B3, 2.7B3 etc.)

Make a note of the source of the title proper if other than the title page:

```
Title from cover
```

3.7.4 Variations in title (AACR2 1.7B4, 2.7B4, etc.)

Note any variations in the title borne by the item or relating to the item, e.g. cover title, spine title. Note also the title of the exhibition where this is known to differ from the title given on the item, where this is not already present as part of the nature, scope, or artistic form note (AACR2 1.7B4, 2.7B4).

```
Val Archer 1998
Title on inside front cover: Val Archer's inaugural show
with Chris Beetles
```

The cataloguer should also make an added title entry:

```
Val Archer's inaugural show with Chris Beetles
```

3.7.5 Parallel titles and other title information (AACR2 1.7B5, 2.7B5, etc.)

Record parallel titles in another language or other title information not already recorded in the title and statement of responsibility area, if deemed important.

> **MLR:** Note the presence of a parallel title in English if this is not given in the title area and supplement this with an added entry for the title in English, if thought to be a useful access point (see Section 6.4.2.8 and associated MLR).

3.7.6 Statements of responsibility (AACR2 1.7B6, 2.7B6, etc.)

Statements of responsibility not appearing "prominently" enough to be added to the title and statement of responsibility area or excluded from it because they relate to production of the catalogue or exhibition or to sponsorship may be given in the notes.

Include here the name of the museum or gallery responsible for organising the exhibition, if not already included in the title and statement of responsibility area.

If the catalogue contains a substantial text and the author's name is not prominent (i.e. not present on title page or title page verso or preliminaries including cover and colophon), include the name here.

The names of other individuals or institutions associated with the exhibition may be made at the discretion of the cataloguing agency, e.g. notes concerning exhibition designers, sponsors etc.

Information included in the title and statement of responsibility area should not be repeated in the notes.

> **MLR:** In cataloguing at this level, it is unlikely that additional statements of responsibility will be included in the notes. However, it is recommended that the name of the institution responsible for the exhibition to which the item relates is entered here if it is not given elsewhere in the record. Where this name is already present in the title and statement of responsibility area or in the publication, distribution area there is no need to repeat it.

3.7.7 Edition and history (AACR2 1.7B7, 2.7B7, etc.)

Include here any explanatory information about the edition in hand and any related edition where this information is available, e.g. give details of differences in the reproductions or the works included where known (see also Section 3.3).

```
Chance, choice and irony : Mac Adams, Colin Crumplin, Joel
Fisher ...

Published in conjunction with an exhibition held at the
John Hansard Gallery, Southampton University, 26 Apr.-11
June 1994. First exhibited in reduced form at the Todd
Gallery, London, 24 Feb.- 2 Apr. 1994
```

> **MLR:** Notes on edition and history should be made as required by the cataloguing agency.

3.7.8 Publication, distribution, etc. (AACR2 1.7B9, 2.7B9, etc.)

Where a publication is known to have been issued in parallel, for example by each of the venues hosting the exhibition, state this in order to clarify the relationship between different publications associated with the same event.

> **MLR:** Notes on the publication or distribution of an item need only be made at the discretion of the cataloguing agency.

3.7.9 Physical description (AACR2 1.7B10, 2.7B10, etc.)

Add any further details regarded as significant.

```
Limited ed. of 60 numbered copies
```

3.7.10 Accompanying material (AACR2 1.7B11, 2.7B11, etc.)

Note here any accompanying private view card or separate list of works unless already recorded in the physical description area.

```
Accompanied by typescript list of exhibits

Includes loose-leaf price-list inserted
```

3.7.11 Other formats (AACR2 1.7B16, 2.7B16, etc.)

Make a note if the contents of the item are available in an alternative physical form, e.g.

```
Issued in parallel on CD-ROM
```

> **MLR**: No note need be given unless the cataloguing agency wants to make a connection to another item in its own collection.

3.7.12 Contents (AACR2 1.7B18, 2.7B18, etc.)

Give the titles of individual catalogues where an item has a collective title and individual items contained within it, e.g.

[example still needed]

3.7.13 Copy being described, Library's holdings, etc. (AACR2 1.7B20, 2.7B20, etc.)

Note anything significant about the particular copy being described. Include here any significant details relating to provenance of the item.

```
Library's copy is no. 135

Signed by the artist
```

3.8 Standard number and terms of availability area (AACR2 1.8, 2.8, etc.)

Include an International Standard Book Number (ISBN) or other standard number and note the presence of alternative ISBNs for alternative binding or formats, e.g. paperback, overseas publisher. Give the International Standard Serial Number (ISSN) where present on a serial item.

> **MLR**: Always record the ISBN of the item in hand if it is not present elsewhere in the record.

PART II

CHOICE AND FORM OF ACCESS POINTS

4. Introduction to main and added entries

These guidelines correspond to AACR2 Part II Headings, Uniform Titles and References, in particular to the rules contained in Chapter 21 Choice of access points.[11]

> "In Part II the rules are based on the proposition that one *main entry* is made for each item described, and that this is supplemented by *added entries*" – (AACR2 0.5)

Although acknowledging that the distinction between main and added entries is less significant in an automated catalogue, Chapter 21 of AACR2 sets out detailed rules for establishing main entry and this concept remains fundamental within the code.[12]

5. Establishing access points

During the process of describing the item, various names will have emerged in association with it. These may include personal names such as artists and authors and the names of corporate bodies such as the institution responsible for organising the exhibition or the museum or gallery acting as the venue. In a few cases, the exhibition may be regarded as an independent corporate event rather like a conference and as such the name of exhibition may acquire the status of a corporate entity in its own right. This section sets out the steps involved in identifying these access points, followed in Section 6 by a discussion of each type of heading. Guidance on the number and form of added entries is also included.

In determining access points the cataloguer must:

5.1 Identify those persons or corporate bodies responsible for the intellectual or artistic content of the item

5.2 Determine the appropriate placing of primary intellectual or creative responsibility and assign the main entry by following the rules set out in AACR2 Chapter 21

5.3 Assign access points for the other names identified

5.4 Determine the appropriate form of each of the headings assigned as an access point

---

[11] Note that in AACR2, the term access point is used almost synonymously with heading although in fact access point may be considered to be a broader term as it includes the title (which is not generally considered to be a heading).

[12] AACR2 0.5 emphasises the continuing significance of main entry in making single entry lists and in establishing a single citation for a work.

> **MLR**: In minimum level cataloguing bibliographic description is necessarily abbreviated and MLR records are likely to include fewer of the access points covered by the provisions below. All headings assigned by the cataloguer must be identified and constructed with the same care as for full level cataloguing.
>
> In some cases the description justifying inclusion of a heading may be schematic. An added entry for the exhibition venue, for example may be assigned on the basis of a corporate name given in the publication, distribution area.

6. Rules governing choice of main entry (AACR2 Chapter 21)

AACR2 Chapter 21 provides detailed rules for determining the main entry heading under which an item should be entered. Added entries are covered by AACR2 21.6 and further guidance is provided in Section 7 below. The following sections should be read in conjunction with the flowchart given at APPENDIX C.

To apply the rules correctly, the cataloguer must first have a clear understanding of the definitions of personal author and corporate body:

6.1 Definition of personal author

"... the person chiefly responsible for the creation of the intellectual or artistic content of a work. ..." -- (AACR2 21.1A1)

6.2 Definition of a corporate body

" ... an organization or a group of persons that is identified by a particular name and that acts, or may act, as an entity. Consider a corporate body to have a name if the words referring to it are a specific appellation rather than a general description. Consider a body to have a name if, in a script and language using capital letters for proper names, the initial letters of the words referring to it are consistently capitalized, and/or if, in a language using articles, the words are always associated with a definite article. Typical examples of corporate bodies are associations, institutions, business firms, non-profit enterprises, governments, government agencies, projects and programmes, religious bodies, local church groups identified by the name of the church, and conferences. ..." -- AACR2 21.1B1

The rule goes on:

"Consider ad hoc events (such as athletic contests, exhibitions, expeditions, fairs, and festivals) and vessels (e.g. ships and spacecraft) to be corporate bodies."

6.3   Criteria for main entry under name of corporate body

Corporate bodies associated with the exhibition and its catalogue fall into a number of distinct types, each of which will be dealt with in detail below. For the name of a corporate body to be considered as main entry, the exhibition catalogue must meet certain other criteria set out in AACR2 21.1B2.

6.3.1   The work must emanate from the corporate body

"Consider a work to emanate ... if it is issued by that body *or* ...caused to be issued by that body *or* ... originated with that body" – (AACR2 21.1B2 Footnote)

This is generally interpreted to mean that the body must be named as the publisher in the publication, distribution area or have caused the work to be published as indicated by the presence of wording such as "Published for" or "on behalf of" the organisation concerned.

```
Tate Gallery
From Turner's studio : paintings and oil sketches from the
Turner Bequest / David Blayney Brown
London : Tate Gallery, 1991
```

In this example, Tate Gallery is assigned main entry because the objects exhibited form part of the Gallery's collection and the catalogue was published by and for the Gallery. The author and artist are assigned as added entries.

```
Brown, David Blayney
Turner, J. M. W. (Joseph Mallord William), 1775-1851
```

6.3.2 The publication must fall into one of the categories listed in AACR2 21.1B2

Categories a) or d) are most likely to be applicable when dealing with exhibition documentation:

"a) those [publications] of an administrative nature dealing with
    the corporate body itself
    or its internal policies, procedures, finances, and/or
    operations
    or its officers, staff and/or membership (e.g. directories)
    or **its resources (e.g. catalogues, inventories)**"

"d) those [publications] that report the collective activity of a
    conference ..., of an expedition ..., **or of an event (e.g. an
    exhibition**, fair, festival) **falling within the definition of**

> a corporate body ... provided that the ... event is
> prominently named ... in the item being catalogued"

For printed publications, the event is only "prominently named" if it appears in one of the following places: title page, other preliminaries (defined as verso of title page(s), any pages preceding the title page(s) or cover) or colophon (AACR2 0.8 and AACR2 2.0B Prescribed sources of information). To identify the prescribed sources to be used in cataloguing other formats follow AACR2 0.8 and the prescribed sources specified within the relevant chapter of AACR2 Part I. Description.

6.3.3 Multiple statements of responsibility: selecting the correct main entry

Multiple statements of responsibility occur frequently in exhibition catalogues and the cataloguer will almost always have to make a choice between names when identifying the main entry. Note, for example that a named corporate body meeting the criteria for entry under corporate body takes precedence over a personal name associated with the item. Use the flow chart at APPENDIX C in conjunction with relevant sections below as an indication of the preferred hierarchy.

6.4   Corporate body as main entry

6.4.1 Name of exhibition (AACR2 21.1B1, AACR2 21.1B2)

The inclusion of "ad hoc events ... such as ... exhibitions" in the definition of corporate body opens up the possibility that an exhibition name may stand as a corporate entity in its own right entered under its own name. However, for this to occur, the exhibition name must meet the conditions established by the definition at AACR2 21.1B1 (Section 6.2 above). Note that:

i) The exhibition must be prominently named in the item in hand (as defined in AACR2 0.8)

ii) The publication must emanate from the named exhibition as given in the heading

iii) The publication must fall under the definition of AACR2 21.1B2 d) in reporting the "collective activity" of the exhibition (i.e. in providing a record of the event in the form of a catalogue) or in setting out the financial or administrative details associated with mounting the exhibition (AACR2 21.1B2 a)).

Do not infer the name of the exhibition from the title of the item. Look out for other clues such as the name consistently capitalised not simply as a typographic device, use of the definite article, etc.

Following these rules, certain large, national or international exhibitions should be entered under name of the exhibition as an event, e.g. Great Exhibition, Festival of Britain. This is because they clearly "emanate" from the exhibition and have an exhibition name prominently identified on the item and well established in reference sources.

```
National Exhibition of Arts, Manufactures, and Materials of
Ireland (1852 : Cork, Ireland)
```

In most other cases assigning exhibition name as main entry is less than straightforward and requires careful interpretation by the cataloguer to determine when the exhibition can be regarded as "prominently named". This is a grey area and the extent to which exhibition titles are established as names differs between cataloguing agencies.[13] It is hoped that the compilation of these guidelines will re-open discussion of the difficulties caused by this particular aspect of the code and will lead to revision.

It should be noted that the Library of Congress restricts the occurrence of name of exhibition as main entry by means of an LC Rule Interpretation relating to AACR2 21.1.B1:

```
"In general, consider named ad hoc events of the types listed ...
to be corporate bodies. However, for art exhibitions, treat as
corporate bodies only those that recur under the same name (e.g.
Biennale di Venezia, Documenta)"[14]
```

Although statements of frequency, e.g. triennial, may on occasion provide further evidence that the exhibition has a recognised name established by repetition, AACR2 does not include this proviso and it is certainly possible to establish a one-off exhibition as event under its own name. It is not necessarily the case that an exhibition must recur for it to be considered a candidate for entry under its own name.

Exhibition-related publications that record the organisation, administration and financial dealings associated with mounting the exhibition are far less frequently encountered but on occasion may be established under exhibition name following AACR2 21.1B2 category a).

For instructions on the form of exhibition name entry see Section 8.3.1.

6.4.2 Other corporate names (AACR2 21.1B2a and AACR2 21.4B)

6.4.2.1 Name of museum or gallery

Having established that the exhibition is not named in the sense established by the AACR2 definition and/or that the publication fails to meet the criteria for exhibition name entry, the cataloguer must determine whether the publication should be entered under any other corporate name associated with the event. Where museum and gallery names are

---

[13]   It should be noted that the extent to which this type of entry is made differs between the national cataloguing agencies. The British Library is generous in its interpretation of what constitutes an ad hoc named exhibition; the National Art Library is more cautious. The Library of Congress follows its own rule interpretation to restrict the use of exhibition name main entry. Librarians and users need to be aware of these differences in making use of library catalogues or in downloading records.

[14]   Library of Congress Rule Interpretations. Washington, D.C.: Cataloging Distribution Service, 1990- 21.1B1 (Nov. 1995.) p.2

associated with the exhibition, the same criteria set out in AACR2 21.1B2 should be applied to determine whether main entry should be given to the institution (see Sections 6.3.1 and 6.3.2).

The publication must emanate from the institution (i.e. be issued by, or caused to be issued by, or originate with the institution).

It must fall into one of the categories specified in AACR2 21.1B2. In the case of an institution associated with an exhibition, the publication is most likely to be covered by AACR2 21.1B2 category a) The works covered in the exhibition must belong to the corporate body from which the publication emanates and the item must present itself as a catalogue, e.g.

```
Victoria and Albert Museum
A grand design: the art of the Victoria and Albert Museum /
Malcolm Baker, Brenda Richardson, editors. -- London : V&A
Publications with the Baltimore Museum of Art, 1997.
Catalogue of an exhibition held at the Baltimore Museum of
Art and other museums in North America, 1997-1999 and at the
Victoria and Albert Museum, 1999-2000
```

This publication is entered under Victoria and Albert Museum because it emanates from (is published by) the Museum, and it contains works drawn from the Museum's permanent collection.

The name of a museum or gallery holding and organising an exhibition cannot be assigned as main entry if the works in the exhibition are borrowed from elsewhere. Thus in very many cases the names of museums and galleries associated with the exhibition are given as added entries (see Section 7.2.5).

```
Beyond reason : art and psychosis : works from the Prinzhorn
collection. -- London : Hayward Gallery, 1996
```

In the above example, a catalogue of a loan exhibition held at the gallery, title main entry is assigned because the works exhibited are drawn from various other collections.

Examples included at AACR2 21.4A1 and AACR2 21.4B1 illustrate that corporate name takes precedence over personal name where the conditions of AACR2 21.1B2 are met. Further evidence of this priority can be found at AACR2 21.17 Reproductions of two or more art works. This rule refers the cataloguer back to AACR2 21.1B2a for works emanating from a corporate body that are catalogues of the holdings of that body. From this it can be seen that corporate name main entry must always be ruled out before the cataloguer considers name of author or artist as a potential main entry.

```
Tate Gallery
Young Turner: early work to 1800: watercolours and drawings
from the Turner Bequest 1787-1900 / Anne Lyles. -- London:
Tate Gallery, 1989
```

In the above example, main entry is given to the institution because the publication emanates from the Tate Gallery and contains works derived from the permanent collection. Added entries are made for the author and artist.[15]

```
Lyles, Anne
Turner, J. M. W. (Joseph Mallord William), 1775-1851
```

The presence or absence of reproductions of the artist's work and/or text about the artist has no bearing upon this choice.

```
Kent, Sarah
Shark infested waters : the Saatchi Collection of British art
in the 90s. -- London : Zwemmer, 1994
```

In the above example, main entry is given to the author of the text with the Saatchi Collection assigned an added entry because the publication does not "emanate" from the Collection.

6.4.2.2 Exhibitions derived from stock: corporate name main entry under dealer's name

Exhibitions derived from the collections of art dealers may also fulfil the criteria for corporate name main entry (under company name). Where an exhibition is drawn from the stock of an art dealer and is exhibited for sale, enter under the corporate name providing that the item in hand meets the criteria at AACR2 21.1B2. The item must emanate from (be published by) the dealer and the items contained in the publication must be derived from the stock of the particular company. The publication must also present itself as a catalogue, e.g.

```
Joseph Fach (Firm)
Malerei und Zeichnung : deutsche Kunstler im 19. Jahrhundert.
-- Frankfurt-am-Main : Joseph Fach, [1992]. Dealer's
catalogue
```

6.4.2.3 Exhibitions emanating from named societies and associations

A further type of corporate name main entry is something of a hybrid. It concerns those named societies of artists holding regular exhibitions of work by their members and issuing catalogues. These generally fall under the provisions of AACR2 21.1B2 a) as they deal with both membership and the resources of a particular society. They are also covered by AACR2 21.1B2 d) in reporting the collective activity of a prominently named exhibition, e.g.

---

[15]   The British Library and National Library of Canada give corporate name priority as set out in AACR2. The Library of Congress however, applies this order of precedence only where a catalogue covers the works of two or more artists. For works associated with a single artist a Library of Congress Rule Interpretation is invoked, instructing entry under name of artist. Once again this causes differences in the resulting catalogue records.

```
Society of Wood Engravers. Annual Exhibition (56th : 1993-94
: London, England)
56th Annual Exhibition, 1993-4 / the Society of Wood
Engravers
[Richmond-upon-Thames : The Society, 1993]
```

6.4.2.4 Exhibitions of students' work

Corporate main entry for exhibitions of the work of students forming part of end of year shows also comes under the provision of AACR2 21.1B2 d) as the collective activity of an event, e.g.

```
Royal College of Art
Royal College of Art painting degree show 1992.
[London : Royal College of Art, 1992].
```

6.5 Personal name as main entry

If the conditions for corporate name main entry are not present, the cataloguer should move on to consider whether the publication falls within the AACR2 definition of personal authorship.

```
"... the person chiefly responsible for the creation of the
intellectual or artistic content of a work. ..."  -- (AACR2 21.1A1)
```

```
"Enter a work, a collection of works, or selections from a work
or works by one personal author ... under the heading for that
person whether named in the item being catalogued or not."  --
(AACR2 21.4A1)
```

In the case of exhibition documentation the apparent simplicity of the second paragraph of this rule is qualified by supplementary rules for items containing reproductions of two or more art works at AACR2 21.17.

Supplementary rules for works containing reproductions

21.17A Without text

21.17A1 Enter a work consisting of reproductions of the works of an artist without accompanying text under the heading for the artist.

21.17B With text

21.17B1 If a work consists of reproductions of the works of an artist and text about the artist and/or the works reproduced, enter under the heading appropriate to the text if the person who

```
wrote  it  is  represented  as  author  in  the  chief  source  of
information  of  the  item  being  catalogued.  Make  an  added  entry
under  the  heading  for  the  artist.  Otherwise,  enter  under  the
heading  for  the  artist.  In  case  of  doubt,  enter  under  the  heading
for  the  artist.

If  the  work  is  entered  under  the  heading  for  the  artist,  make  an
added  entry  under  the  heading  for  the  person  who  wrote  the  text
if  his  or  her  name  appears  in  the  chief  source  of  information.
..."
```

The interrelationship between these rules can cause confusion by adding a further factor, the presence or absence of reproductions, to the selection of a personal name as main entry. However once corporate name main entry has been ruled out it should be noted that the presence of a named author in the chief source of information will almost always takes precedence.

6.5.1 Author of text (AACR2 21.17B)

Where a work includes text, and the writer of the text is represented as the author in the chief source of information, the publication should be entered under the name of the author (following AACR2 21.17B). Note that this applies only to significant statements of authorship, and not to editors or compilers. Where the names present in the chief source are names of editors or compilers they should be assigned as added entries.

Where an individual is named on the title page but the nature of the contribution is unclear, the addition of an explanatory phrase to clarify the nature of responsibility may in certain cases indicate that main entry under author's name is inappropriate, e.g.

```
      [captions] by
or    [accompanying text] by
```

In such cases the name should be assigned as an added entry.

If responsibility is shared between two or three authors and principal responsibility is attributed by wording or layout to one of the authors named, this person should be given main entry even if the name does not appear first on the title page. If principal responsibility is not attributed to any of the authors by wording or layout, enter under the heading for the first named (AACR2 21.6C1).

In a work containing two or more reproductions, an author named outside the chief source of information cannot be given main entry (AACR2 21.17B1).

In case of doubt, the rule instructs entry under artist.

6.5.2 Artist's name (AACR2 21.17)

If the chief source of information includes no statement of authorship relating to text, entry under artist's name should be considered. Artist as main entry may be assigned under the provisions of AACR2 21.1A1 and AACR2 21.4A1 where the artist is named on the title page as the single or principal person responsible for the intellectual or artistic content of the publication, regardless of the presence or absence of reproductions. In other cases, an artist's name may be given in the title to indicate the subject of the catalogue. In such cases, selection of artist as main entry is based upon the presence of two or more reproductions of art works within the catalogue and the absence of a statement in the chief source assigning responsibility to the author of any text (following AACR2 21.17B1).

6.5.2.1 Exhibition of the work of a single artist

Exhibition catalogues concerned with the work of a single artist and containing two or more reproductions should be entered under the name of the artist once entry under an author has been ruled out (i.e. no author of text is given in the chief source).

Note the proviso at AACR2 21.17B "In case of doubt, enter under the heading for the artist".

Where the catalogue contains two or more reproductions of a single artist's work but no text (interpreted to mean no significant text beyond brief captions for the works) then the publication should also be entered under artist's name (following AACR2 21.17A quoted above).

For guidance on how to treat artists working under a shared pseudonym or a collective name, see Section 8.2.

6.5.2.2 Exhibition of the work of multiple artists

Where no author is named in the chief source and the exhibition covers the work of two or three artists (responsible for the artistic/intellectual content) then the work may be considered to fall under the definition of "shared responsibility" given at AACR2 21.6. The main entry should be assigned to the principal or first named artist with added entries under the second (and the third named where present).

Note that the reproductions rule as set out in AACR2 21.17B applies only to publications concerned with the work of a single artist.

In all other cases apply the provisions of AACR2 21.7 when dealing with exhibitions including the work of more than three contributing artists. This rule covers collections of works by different persons or bodies and instructs the cataloguer to give the title as main entry, making added entries for compilers, editors and, where the work covers no more than three artists, for the named artists.[16]

However if the item lacks a collective title, the main entry reverts once again to the artist responsible for the first named work. In determining whether the publication has a collective title take account of the rules for items with multiple title pages given at AACR2 1.0H (see Section 3.1.2).

6.5.2.3 Exhibitions containing one reproduction

Where an exhibition catalogue includes a single reproduction of an artist's work together with text, it is not covered by AACR2 21.16B and yet does not fall within AACR2 21.17, which covers works containing two or more reproductions. Enter the publication under the heading for the author of text where the author's name is given in the chief source, making an added entry for the name of the artist.

It is recommended that entry should be made under the name of the artist if no author of text is given.

This follows the principle established by AACR2 21.16 and AACR2 21.17.[17]

6.6 Title main entry (AACR2 21.1C)

Where a work does not fall into any of the categories for corporate main entry given at AACR2 21.1B2, includes no statement of responsibility in the chief source and is not an illustrated catalogue of works by up to three artists, enter it under title. If it emanates from a corporate body with no specified name, enter it under title (AACR2 21.5A).

Title main entry should be given following AACR2 21.7B1. If, however, the item lacks a collective title page, enter under the heading appropriate to the first bibliographic work in the item (AACR2 21.7C1).

---

[16]   Although as noted previously further added entries may be made at the discretion of the cataloguing agency for exhibitions including the work of more than three artists.

[17]   AACR2 21.16B is also concerned with the main entry for a single reproduction of an artwork. The rule instructs entry under the person assigned responsibility for the original work (the artist). This rule is phrased in such a way that it appears to apply only to single and separate reproductions and not to the exhibition catalogue containing text and a single reproduction. This type of catalogue does not appear to be covered easily by the provisions of either AACR2 rule.

7. Rules governing choice of added entries (AACR2 21.29, 21.30)

7.1 General rules

"Make added entries to provide access to bibliographic descriptions in addition to the access provided by the main entry heading." -- (AACR2 21.29A)

General rules for the creation of added entries are set out in AACR2 21.29 and specific rules in AACR2 21.30. Added entries may be made for names of persons, corporate bodies and titles.

The provision for making added entries is generous and gives the cataloguer virtual carte blanche to make any additional access points required by the cataloguing agency.

"In addition, make an added entry under the heading for a person or a corporate body or under a title if some catalogue users might suppose that the description of an item would be found under that heading or title ..." – (AACR2 21.29C)

It may be difficult to determine how many added entries to make when multiple statements of responsibility are associated with the exhibition catalogue. The "rule of three" governing the number of names included in the description of the item (within the statement of responsibility) may be used as a guide. AACR2 instructs that up to three names may be given in any separate statement of responsibility. Where more than three persons or bodies are present (relating to the same kind of responsibility), only the first named is given. This same rule of three may be used to determine the number of added entries. Where one, two or three persons or bodies share responsibility of a particular type, each name may be given an access point. Where four or more names are present in a single statement, it is essential to give the first name an added entry. The other names may be omitted.

Exhibition catalogues frequently include several separate statements of responsibility naming persons or bodies performing different functions in relation to the catalogue and exhibition and the cataloguer should apply the rule of three to each of these statements. Thus an exhibition catalogue will frequently have more than three added entries associated with different kinds of contribution.

Given that AACR2 21.29C quoted above, AACR2 21.29D and AACR2 21.30H allow the cataloguing agency freedom to make almost any added entries deemed useful, the cataloguer should not feel constrained if further access points are felt to be needed.

"If, in the context of a given catalogue, an added entry is required under a heading or title other than those prescribed in 21.30, make it." -- AACR2 21.29D

"Make an added entry under the heading for any other name that would provide an important access point ..." -- AACR2 21.30H1

MLR: At minimum level, added entries are likely to be fewer in number because the catalogue entry is necessarily more schematic. In certain cases the justification for the inclusion of an added entry may be less obvious to the catalogue user as the role of the named person or corporate body given in a heading and present in the description may not be explicitly stated.

7.2 Specific rules

AACR2 21.30 sets out specific rules for different types of contribution to the item. Note that the rule of three described above applies to all the separate types of added entry described by .

"If the following subrules refer to only one person or corporate body and two or three persons or bodies are involved in a particular instance, make added entries under the headings for each. If four or more persons or bodies are involved in a particular instance, make an added entry when appropriate under the heading for the one named first in the source from which the names are taken."

7.2.1 Collaborators (AACR2 21.30B)

If the main entry is given to the first named of two or three collaborating persons or bodies named in a statement of responsibility, make added entries for the second and third named collaborators.

If the main entry is given to the heading for a corporate body or under title, make added entries for up to three collaborating persons or bodies, or under the first named of four or more. Other related persons or bodies may still be given access points if they are considered sufficiently important by the cataloguing agency (see AACR2 21.30F).

7.2.2 Authors of text (AACR2 21.30C, AACR2 21.30F)

AACR2 21.30C instructs that an added entry should be made for a prominently named author of text (i.e. named on title page, other preliminaries - verso of title page, pages preceding the title page or cover). The writer of significant text may be given an added entry even where the name does not appear "prominently" if it is felt to be an important additional access point e.g. if the writer is responsible for the only significant text in a catalogue (following AACR2 21.30F). There is no need to make an added entry if the contribution is minor, e.g. writer of foreword and they are not named in the chief source.

> **MLR**: The authors named in the first statement of responsibility should be included as a minimum requirement. The first named author will depend on the sequence or layout of the chief source (AACR2 1.1F6):
>
> ```
> Slivka, Rose
> The art of Peter Voulkos / Rose Slivka and Karen Tsujimoto
> ```
>
> Thus an added entry will be made for:
>
> ```
> Tsujimoto, Karen
> ```
>
> With a further entry for the artist's name:
>
> ```
> Voulkos, Peter
> ```
>
> Any additional authors can be included at the discretion of the cataloguing agency, if judged to be useful access points (see AACR2 21.30F).

7.2.3 Artists

The text of AACR2 21.30H continues:

"Make an added entry under the heading for any other name that would provide an important access point unless the relationship between the name and the work is purely that of a subject. ..."

Follow this rule in making added entries for artists' names. AACR2 21.17B1 also specifically instructs that in works containing two or more reproductions, the artist's name should be included as an added entry where it has not been assigned main entry.

On the analogy of the rule of three included at AACR2 21.30A1, up to three prominently named artists, or the first-named only of a larger number, should be given added entries. Follow the specific guidance given under contributors above:

```
Cage, John
Dancers on a plane / John Cage, Merce Cunningham, Jasper
Johns
```

In this example, main entry is given to the first named with added entries assigned to the remaining names:

```
Cunningham, Merce
Johns, Jasper
```

Exhibition catalogues frequently list many named artists on the title page, often in no other priority than alphabetical order. Cataloguing agencies may choose to use the licence of AACR2 21.29D to establish a more generous policy, according to need and resources.

Added entries for artists do not usually require justification from the body of the description but a note may be made if required. It may be useful to provide a note where the cataloguing agency chooses to make a heading for specific artists excluded from the title and/or statement of responsibility area.

> **MLR:** Up to three prominently named artists, or the first named only of a larger number, should be given added entries.

7.2.4 Editors and compilers (AACR2 21.30D)

Make an added entry for the editor or compiler of an item provided that these names appear prominently (i.e. named on title page, other preliminaries - verso of title page, pages preceding the title page or cover). Apply the "rule of three" to any statement concerned with compilation or editorial responsibility.

Take particular care in dealing with statements concerned with consultant editors or with persons whose contribution is limited to the physical production of the book, such as production editors, as these names do not generally require added entries.

```
Contemporary Russian artists : exhibition and catalogue /
edited and introduced by Amnon Barzel, Claudia Jolles
```

Title main entry is given here, with added entries for:

```
Barzel, Amnon
Jolles, Claudia
```

7.2.5. Corporate bodies (AACR2 21.30E)

"Make an added entry under the heading for a prominently named corporate body, unless it functions solely as distributor or manufacturer. ..." – (AACR2 21.30E)

Follow this rule to make added entries for the exhibition venues, for the lending institution and/or for any other corporate name associated with the item not already given an entry under the collaborators rule. Where several bodies share responsibility, for example as exhibition organisers or venues, make added entries for up to three (following AACR2 21.30A1). If more than three venues are listed, make an added entry under the first named and/or any further venues of particular interest to the cataloguing agency.

Although AACR2 21.30E1 specifies that a prominently named corporate body may be assigned an added entry, AACR2 21.30F1 goes on to instruct the cataloguer to:

"Make an added entry under the heading for a person or corporate body having a relationship to a work not treated in 21.1-21.28 if the heading provides an important access point(e.g. ... a museum in which an exhibition is held)."

Thus an exhibition venue would generally be assigned as a heading regardless of the prominence rule at AACR2 21.30E1 .

MLR: An added entry should be made for the first-named exhibition venue (AACR2 21.30F1). Added entries for further venues are not required unless a subsequently named museum or gallery has a particular significance for the cataloguing agency, or the institution concerned has done more than simply host the exhibition.

> Medieval manuscripts on Merseyside : catalogue of an exhibition held in the University Art Gallery, Liverpool, from May 6 to 16 July 1993, and in the Courtauld Institute Galleries, London, from 15 October to 28 November 1993

Title main entry is given here, with an added entry for the first venue:

University of Liverpool. Art Gallery

Where the item describes a travelling exhibition derived from the collection of one or more institutions, give exhibition, corporate or personal author, artist or title main entry as appropriate, with added entries for the originating institution and the first or most significant venue if not present as main entry.

```
Hearne, Thomas, 1744-1817
Thomas Hearne 1744-1817 : watercolours and drawings : a catalogue
of a touring exhibition held at Bolton
Museum and Art Gallery, 17 August  28 September 1995,
Southampton Art Gallery, 2 November  8th December 1995, Victoria
Art Gallery, Bath, 14 December 1995  11th January 1996 ... /
exhibition organised by David Morris ; catalogue entries by David
Morris.


Morris, David
Bolton Museum and Art Gallery
```

Artist's name is given main entry, with added entries for David Morris, and the first named venue. There is no mention of the originating institution in the bibliographic description and hence no entry has been made; however, if the name of the originating institution had been recorded then it would have been appropriate to provide an access point.

7.2.6 Named exhibitions

Added entries may occasionally be required for named exhibitions when the name can be established but does not appear prominently on the item. In other cases the title of a related exhibition mentioned in the preface, introduction or text may differ from the title of the publication in hand, e.g. a revised or updated catalogue of an exhibition held under a variant title. In such cases an exhibition name added entry should be made.

The reasons for the entry should be clear from the catalogue description, most often explained in a note, e.g.

```
A guide to the location of the fine and decorative art
collections of Ernest E. Cook

"Updated guide published as a companion to the catalogue
for the exhibition A Gift to the Nation: the Fine and
Decorative Art Collections of Ernest E. Cook, held at the
Holburne Museum and Crafts Study Centre, Bath, 16 May - 1
Sept. 1991" - t.p. verso
```

The above example should be given an exhibition name added entry because it does not meet the criteria for main entry under exhibition name.

```
Gift to the Nation (Exhibition : 1991 : Holburne Museum
and Crafts Study Centre)
```

For further instructions on the construction of the exhibition name heading see Section 8.3.1.

7.2.7 Added entries for other persons and corporate bodies

Added entries may also be made for the names of authors/ artists on the staff of the cataloguing agency's own institution, exhibition curators not otherwise assigned a heading, prominently named organising bodies or sponsors without intellectual or artistic responsibility for the work but nevertheless considered likely to be sought (AACR2 21.30D1, AACR2 21.30E1)

Where a contribution is concerned with the physical production of the book, designers, production editors, etc. added entries are not usually made although once again this is at the discretion of the cataloguing agency and there are exceptions. Significant contributions may require added entries. Added entries should be made for named designers where the catalogue design is particularly significant, e.g. designed by an artist represented in the exhibition.

Where an author's name is followed by the name of a sponsor or employer, the name of sponsor or employer is not usually given an added entry.

In some cases a corporate name appearing as publisher and present only in the publication, distribution area of the description has more involvement with the item than simply publishing or co-publishing it. In such circumstances, an added entry may be given. This is at the discretion of the cataloguing agency and does not require justification from the body of the description.

```
London: Wimbledon School of Art in association with Tate
Gallery, 1994
```

Translators should not usually be given an access point (but note the exceptions in AACR2 21.30K1).

7.2.8 Title added entries (AACR2 21.30J)

```
"Make an added entry under the title proper of every item
entered under a personal heading, a corporate heading, or a
uniform title ..." (AACR2 21.30J1)
```

No added entry should be made if the title proper is essentially the same as the main entry heading or a reference to that heading, e.g. the item has been given an exhibition name as main entry and this is identical to the title.

No added entry should be made where the title proper has been composed by the cataloguer (and is therefore most unlikely to be sought as an access point).
AACR2 21.30J includes further exceptions.

Added title entries may also be required for any alternative, parallel or variant title found on the item.

8. Form of heading (AACR2 Chapters 22-24)

8.1 Introduction

Name headings should be established following the rules set out in AACR2 Chapters 22-24. These rules are not repeated here except where necessary to identify underlying principles and/or to expand upon points specific to exhibition documentation.

Headings constructed according to AACR2 are also generally authority controlled against a local or shared authority file to maintain consistency. The use of international authority files for validation of headings is advised for any library making use of external records. This assists the catalogue user searching across multiple catalogues. The name authority files available from the British Library and Library of Congress are in the process of being combined to form a single integrated file of authorised headings, this *Anglo-American Authority File* (AAAF) is strongly recommended as a source for name authority checking.

For the names of artists, standard reference sources may also need to be consulted. One particularly useful source for verifying artists' names is the *Union List of Artists' Names* (ULAN) which forms part of the Getty Vocabulary Program. It is freely available over the Internet at: <http://shiva.pub.getty.edu/ulan_browser/>

8.2 Headings for persons

AACR2 Chapter 22 provides detailed guidance on how to establish the correct form of a personal name. It provides guidance on the choice between variants of the same name, how to deal with name changes and multiple names (AACR2 22.2). Rules to assist identification of the entry element (AACR2 22.4-22.11) are also included together with detailed guidance on additions to names (AACR2 22.12-22.16) and rules to distinguish otherwise identical names (AACR2 22.17-22.20)

The basic principle underpinning the choice of personal name heading is set out in AACR2 22.1A:

"In general, choose, as the basis of the heading for a person, the name by which he or she is commonly known. This may be the person's real name, pseudonym, title of nobility, nickname, initials, or other appellation."

The name by which a person is "commonly known" is generally determined from the chief sources of information of bibliographic works by that person (AACR2 22.1B). This is less straightforward where the individual is responsible for art works:

"If the person works in a non-verbal context (e.g., a painter, a sculptor) ... determine the name by which he or she is commonly known from reference sources issued in his or her language or country of residence ... " (AACR2 22.1B)

In fact most artists' names are relatively straightforward to establish from the item in hand together with other secondary literature associated with the exhibition. As indicated above it is advisable to check names against an established authority source and to consult biographical reference works in case of doubt.

Pseudonyms are encountered fairly frequently, they are covered in detail in AACR2 22.2B. Collective names used in collaborative work may also be encountered, e.g. Karen Eliot shared by Stewart Home and Pete Horobin among others.

Add an explanatory term as a qualifier if a name is not readily identifiable as the name of a person, e.g.

```
Tourette (artist), fl. 1898-1899
```

8.3 Headings for corporate bodies

"Enter a corporate body directly under the name by which it is commonly identified, except where the rules ... provide for entering it under the name of a higher or related body...or under the name of a government ... "

"Determine the name by which a corporate body is commonly identified from items issued by that body in its language ..., or, when this condition does not apply, from reference sources." -- (AACR2 24.1A)

In establishing the name of a corporate body, AACR2 once again instructs that the body should be entered under the name by which it is "commonly identified". Specific rules are provided for the treatment of name changes (AACR2 24.1C1) of variant names (AACR2 24.2 and AACR2 24.3) and for distinguishing otherwise identical names (AACR2 24.4C). Note especially the rules at AACR2 24.12 for the treatment of subordinate and related bodies. The following additional guidance is provided to assist with certain exhibition-related headings that cause particular problems.

8.3.1 Exhibition name headings

Construct exhibition name headings following AACR2 24.8. Omit from the name of the exhibition terms indicating its number. (AACR2 24.8A1). Instead add the number, date and location in parentheses following the name unless the date and/or location form an integral part of the name in which case leave them in place and do not repeat them in the qualifier. (AACR2 24.8B2)

```
American Exhibition (76th : 1995 : Chicago, Ill.)
```

```
International Health Exhibition (1884 : London, England)

Swansea Festival Exhibition (1992)

Expo 70 (Osaka, Japan)
```

Follow AACR2 24.4B1 and add the designation Exhibition as a qualifier in parentheses following the exhibition name if the nature of the heading is not immediately apparent.

```
Graphica Creativa (Exhibition : 4th : 1984 : Jyväskylä,
Finland)

Britain Can Make It (Exhibition : 1946 : London, England)
```

In some cases Exhibition may appear as a subdivision of the heading for a corporate body, rather than as a qualifier following AACR2 24.13 Type 3.

```
Society of Women Artists. Exhibition (135th : 1996 :
London, England)
```

As indicated above, the exhibition name must still be qualified by number where present and by date and location of the exhibition, as set out in AACR2 24.7 and AACR2 24.8.

If presented with a choice between place name and name of institution as a qualifying location, prefer place name. The name of the institution will generally be given as a separate added entry.

```
Western New York Exhibition (44th : 1992 : Buffalo, N.Y.)
```

The name of the gallery responsible for the exhibition will be entered as an added entry, in this case:

```
Albright-Knox Art Gallery
```

If an exhibition covers more than one year, or has several venues, this can be indicated following the provisions established for conferences (AACR2 24.7B3 and AACR2 24.7B4). These rules should also be applied to named exhibitions.

If a named exhibition is known by more than one form of name, e.g. by an acronym as well as its full form, the cataloguer should establish the predominant form (AACR2 24.1, AACR2 24.2 and AACR2 24.3). In determining the preferred form follow the principle that the heading should be the name by which the exhibition is commonly identified. Make a reference to the preferred form from any variants. Note that where the name of a recurring exhibition changes over time, the provisions of AACR2 24.1C apply and the new form of name should be established as a separate heading linked to any earlier form by cross references.

8.3.2 Names of Museums and Galleries

When the name of a gallery does not convey the idea of a corporate body, add a qualifying term (AACR2 24.4B1).

```
Cornerhouse (Gallery)
```

Such qualifiers are frequently needed when a gallery name includes the personal name of an art dealer or owner. Terms indicating incorporation, e.g. Inc., Ltd. are generally omitted from the name heading unless they are an integral part of the name by virtue of grammatical construction (AACR2 24.5C1). In the absence of a standard abbreviation indicating incorporation, an explanatory designation such as "Firm", "Gallery" may be added (AACR2 24.4B1).

```
Richard Green (Gallery : London, England)
Anthony d'Offay (Firm)
```

In some cases the name of a local place may need to be added to the heading to resolve a conflict between museums or galleries with the same name:

```
Museum of Modern Art (Copenhagen, Denmark)
Museum of Modern Art (New York, N.Y.)
```

In other instances, the place name is an established part of the formal name of the institution, in such cases retain it in the heading and do not repeat it as a qualifier:

```
Tate Gallery Liverpool
Tate Gallery St. Ives
```

9. Uniform titles and cross references (AACR2 Chapters 25 and 26)

Uniform titles are used to bring together all catalogue entries for a work, where different manifestations have appeared under various titles. They may also be used to distinguish two or more works published under identical titles. They are an optional element and are not widely implemented in the cataloguing of exhibition documentation. For detailed rules see AACR2 Chapter 25.

In establishing the correct form of all headings it is essential that references are introduced to guide from non-preferred to the chosen form of name. Follow the detailed provisions of AACR2 Chapter 26 in establishing references.

PART III

SAMPLE CATALOGUE RECORDS

Sample catalogue records

ROYAL COLLEGE OF ART
PAINTING DEGREE SHOW 1992

Darwin Building
Kensington Gore
London SW7 2EU

10th – 20th June
10am to 8pm Daily

ALSO

'OFF SITE'
at the Cooling Gallery
2-4 Cork Street
London W1

3rd to 30th June
10am – 6pm Monday - Friday
10am – 1pm Saturdays

Front cover

Phillip Allen
Matthew Ashby
Richard Clegg **
Kulvinder Kaur Dhew
Milena Dragicevic *
Dan Gardiner
Margarita Gluzberg
Michael Grant
Arabella Johnsen
Debbie Lee
Mao Wen Biao
Sam Morrow
Iain Nicholls
Jiro Osuga
Ian Phillips
Antony Pipe
Karen Robbie *
Keith Roberts
Maggie Roberts *
Michael Robertson
Indrapramit Roy

* No post cards
** Awarded a third year. 'OFF SITE' only.

Back cover

UK MARC

110.20	$aRoyal College of Art (Great Britain)
245.10	$aRoyal College of Art painting degree show 1992
246.30	$aPainting degree show 1992
260.00	$a[London$bRoyal College of Art $c1992]
300.00	$a[17] postcards$ball col. ill.$c15 x 11 cm
500.00	$aPublished on the occasion of the painting degree show held at the RCA, 10-20 June 1992 and at the Cooling Gallery, Cork St., London, 3-30 June 1992
531.00	$aIn a portfolio
610.20	$aRoyal College of Art$xStudents$vExhibitions
710.21	$aCooling Gallery

US MARC

110.2	$aRoyal College of Art (Great Britain).
245.10	$aRoyal College of Art painting degree show 1992.
246.30	$aPainting degree show 1992.
260	$a[London : $bRoyal College of Art, $c1992].
300	$a[17] postcards :$ball col. ill. ;$c15 x 11 cm.
500	$aPublished on the occasion of the painting degree show held at the RCA, 10-20 June 1992 and at the Cooling Gallery, Cork St., London, 3-30 June 1992.
500	$aIn a portfolio.
610.20	$aRoyal College of Art$xStudents$vExhibitions.
710. 2	$aCooling Gallery.

Sample catalogue records

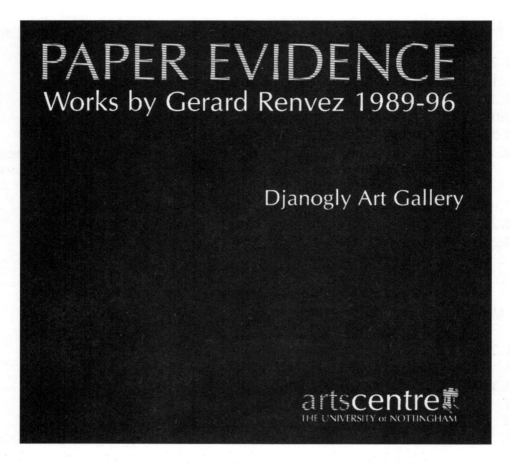

Title page

© 1997 Djanogly Art Gallery
Copyright for essay - Joanne Wright

ISBN 1900809 10 9

Design by David Bickerstaff
at Midlands Arts Marketing Ltd

Printed by Chas. Goater & Son Ltd, Nottingham

Djanogly Art Gallery
The University of Nottingham Arts Centre
University Park
Nottingham NG7 2RD

Extracted from the last page

UK MARC

021.10	$a1900809109$bm
100.10	$aRenvez$hGerard
245.10	$aPaper evidence$bworks by Gerard Renvez 1989-96
260.00	$aNottingham$bDjanogly Gallery$cc1997
300.00	$a16 p.$bcol. ill.$c20 x 22 cm
500.00	$aCatalogue of an exhibition held at the Djanogly Art Gallery in 1997
508.00	$aEssay by Joanne Wright
600.10	$aRenvez$hGerard$vExhibitions
700.11	$aWright$hJoanne
710.21	$aDjanogly Art Gallery

US MARC

020	$a1900809109
100.10	$aRenvez, Gerard.
245.10	$aPaper evidence :$bworks by Gerard Renvez 1989-96.
260	$aNottingham :$bDjanogly Art Gallery,$cc1997.
300	$a16 p. :$bcol. ill. ;$c20 x 22 cm.
500	$aCatalogue of an exhibition held at the Djanogly Art Gallery in 1997.
500	$aEssay by Joanne Wright.
600.10	$aRenvez, Gerard$vExhibitions.
700.1	$aWright, Joanne.
710.2	$aDjanogly Art Gallery.

Sample catalogue records

Richard Serra   Weight and Measure 1992

30 September 1992 – 15 January 1993

Tate Gallery London

Title page

Extracted from the title page verso

UK MARC

021.10	$a1854371096$bm
041.00	$aengger
100.10	$aSerra$hRichard$c1939-
245.10	$aRichard Serra, weight and measure 1992$b30 September - 15 January 1993
246.30	$aWeight and measure 1992
260.00	$aLondon$bTate Gallery Publications$cc1992
300.00	$a111 p.$bill.$i1 port.$c27 cm
500.00	$aExhibition catalogue
504.00	$aIncludes bibliographical references
546.00	$aParallel English and German text
600.10	$aSerra$hRichard$c1939- $vExhibitions
710.21	$aTate Gallery

US MARC

020	$a1854371096
041.0	$aengger
100.1	$aSerra, Richard,$d1939-
245.10	$aRichard Serra, weight and measure 1992 :$b30 September-15 January 1993.
246.30	$aWeight and measure 1992.
260	$aLondon :$bTate Gallery Publications, $cc1992.
300	$a111 p. :$bill., 1 port. ;$c27 cm.
500	$aExhibition catalogue.
504	$aIncludes bibliographical references.
546	$aParallel English and German text.
600.10	$aSerra, Richard,$d1939- $vExhibitions.
710.2	$aTate Gallery.

Sample catalogue records

ROBERT UPSTONE

Turner: The Final Years

WATERCOLOURS 1840–1851

TATE GALLERY

Title page

Cover
A Venetian Fishing Boat 1840
detail (cat.no.3)
ISBN 1 85437 110 X

Published by order of the Trustees 1993
for the exhibition of
10 February – 17 May 1993
Copyright © Tate Gallery 1992 All rights reserved
Designed by Caroline Johnston
Published by Tate Gallery Publications,
Millbank, London SWIP 4RG
Photography by Tate Gallery Photographic Department
Typeset in Baskerville by Apex Computersetting, London
Printed in Great Britain by Balding + Mansell plc,
Wisbech, Cambridgeshire

Extracted from the title page verso

UK MARC

021.10	**$a**185437110X**$b**m
100.10	**$a**Upstone**$h**Robert
245.10	**$a**Turner, the final years**$b**watercolours 1840-1851**$e**Robert Upstone
260.00	**$a**London**$b**Tate Gallery**$c**1993
300.00	**$a**67 p.**$b**ill. (some col.)**$i**ports.**$c**27 cm
500.00	**$a**Published on the occasion of the exhibition held at the Tate Gallery, 10 Feb.-17 May 1993
500.00	**$a**Library's copy donated by the artist
504.00	**$a**Bibliography: p67
600.10	**$a**Turner**$h**J. M. W.**$k**Joseph Mallord William**$c**1775-1851**$v**Exhibitions
700.11	**$a**Turner**$h**J. M. W.**$k**Joseph Mallord William**$c**1775-1851
710.21	**$a**Tate Gallery

US MARC

020	**$a**185437110x
100.1	**$a**Upstone, Robert.
245.10	**$a**Turner, the final years :**$b**watercolours 1840-1851 / **$c**Robert Upstone.
260	**$a**London :**$b**Tate Gallery,**$c**1993.
300	**$a**67 p. :**$b**ill. (some col.), ports. ;**$c**27 cm.
500	**$a**Published on the occasion of the exhibition held at the Tate Gallery, 10 Feb.-17 May 1993.
504	**$a**Bibliography: p. 67.
590	**$a**Library's copy donated by the artist.
600.10	**$a**Turner, J. M. W.**$q**(Joseph Mallord William),**$d**1775-1851 **$v**Exhibitions.
700.1	**$a**Turner, J. M. W.**$q**(Joseph Mallord William),**$d**1775-1851.
710.2	**$a**Tate Gallery.

Sample catalogue records

ONE HUNDRED & THIRTY SEVENTH
ANNUAL INTERNATIONAL
PRINT EXHIBITION
CATALOGUE 1993
SPONSORED BY KODAK

The Royal
Photographic
Society

Title page

Venues

The Royal Photographic Society Bath 20 November - 6 February 9.30 - 5.30pm daily

MAC, Birmingham 16 April - 22 May 1994

Crawford Arts Centre, Fife 3 June - 3 July 1994

Picturehouse, Leicester Mid July - August 1994

Please telephone Bath 0225 462841 to confirm dates

Extracted from the title page verso

UK MARC

111.00	$aAnnual International Print Exhibition$i137th$k1993$jBath, England
245.10	$aOne hundred & thirty seventh Annual International Print Exhibition catalogue, 1993
246.10	$a137th Annual International Print Exhibition catalogue, 1993
260.00	$aBath$bRoyal Photographic Society$c[1993]
300.00	$a64 p.$bill. (chiefly col.)$c30 cm
500.00	$aCatalogue of an exhibition held at the Royal Photographic Society, Bath, 20 Nov. 1993-6 Feb. 1994, at the Midlands Art Centre, Birmingham, 16 Apr.-22 May 1994, at Crawford Arts Centre, Fife, 3 June-3 July 1994 and at the Picture House, Leicester, mid-July-Aug. 1994
514.00	$aSpine title: Royal Photographic Society Annual International Print Exhibition catalogue
710.21	$aRoyal Photographic Society of Great Britain
710.21	$aMidlands Art Centre
710.21	$aCrawford Centre for the Arts
710.21	$aPicture House Gallery
745.10	$aRoyal Photographic Society Annual International Print Exhibition catalogue

US MARC

111.2	$aAnnual International Print Exhibition$n(137th :$d1993 : $cBath, England).
245.10	$aOne hundred & thirty seventh Annual International Print Exhibition catalogue, 1993.
246.33	$a137th Annual International Print Exhibition catalogue, 1993.
246.18	$aRoyal Photographic Society Annual International Print Exhibition catalogue.
260	$aBath :$bRoyal Photographic Society,c[1993].
300	$a64 p. :$bill. (chiefly col.) ;$c30 cm.
500	$aCatalogue of an exhibition held at the Royal Photographic Society, Bath, 20 Nov. 1993-6 Feb. 1994, at the Midlands Art Centre, Birmingham, 16 Apr.-22 May 1994, at Crawford Arts Centre, Fife, 3 June-3 July 1994 and at the Picture House, Leicester, mid-July-Aug. 1994.
710.2	$aRoyal Photographic Society of Great Britain.
710.2	$aMidlands Art Centre.
710.2	$aCrawford Centre for the Arts.
710.2	$aPicture House Gallery.

Sample catalogue records

TATE GALLERY LIVERPOOL CRITICAL FORUM, VOLUME 1

AMERICAN
ABSTRACT EXPRESSIONISM

Editor DAVID THISTLEWOOD
Critical Forum Coordinator ANNE MACPHEE

LIVERPOOL UNIVERSITY PRESS and TATE GALLERY LIVERPOOL

Title page

British Library Cataloguing-in-Publication Data
A British Library CIP Record is available
ISBN 0 85323 338 1

Extracted from the title page verso

UK MARC

021.10	$a0853233381$bm
245.30	$aAmerican abstract expressionism$eeditor, David Thistlewood$ecritical forum coordinator, Anne MacPhee
260.00	$a[Liverpool]$bLiverpool University Press and the Tate Gallery Liverpool$cc1993
300.00	$aviii, 230 p.$bill.$c24 cm
440.00	$aTate Gallery Liverpool critical forum$vv. 1
500.00	$a"American Abstract Expressionism presents contributions made to the conference held in conjunction with the display 'Myth-making: Abstract Expressionist painting from the United States', which was mounted at Tate Gallery Liverpool from March 1992 to January 1993" – Back cover
504.00	$aBibliography: p211-221
700.11	$aThistlewood$hDavid
700.11	$aMacPhee$hAnne
710.21	$aTate Gallery Liverpool
711.00	$aMyth-making$eExhibition$k1992-1993$jLiverpool, England

US MARC

020	$a0853233381
245.00	$aAmerican abstract expressionism /$ceditor, David Thistlewood ; critical forum, coordinator Anne MacPhee.
260	$a[Liverpool] :$bLiverpool University Press and Tate Gallery Liverpool,$cc1993.
300	$aviii, 230 p. :$bill. ;$c24 cm.
440. 0	$aTate Gallery Liverpool critical forum ;$vv. 1
500	$a"American Abstract Expressionism presents contributions made to the conference held in conjunction with the display 'Myth-making: Abstract Expressionist painting from the United States', which was mounted at Tate Gallery Liverpool from March 1992 to January 1993" – Back cover.
504	$aBibliography: p.211-221.
700.1	$aThistlewood, David.
700.1	$aMacPhee, Anne.
710.2	$aTate Gallery Liverpool.
711.2	$aMyth-making (Exhibition)$d(1992-1993$cLiverpool, England).

ANTHONY CARO

New Sculptures · a survey

CARO · FOSTER · WISE

The Millennium Bridge Project

Annely Juda Fine Art
1998

Title page

Designed and typeset by Dalrymple
Printed by BAS Printers Ltd

Published 1998 by Annely Juda Fine Art
© Annely Juda Fine Art, Anthony Caro and the Authors
ISBN 1 870280 66 0

Cover: *The Dreamer's Book* 1995–96
stoneware and steel
29 × 40.5 × 29 cm

Extracted from the title page verso

UK MARC

021.10	$a1870280660$bm
100.10	$aCaro$hAnthony$c1924-
245.10	$aAnthony Caro$bnew sculptures$ba survey$bCaro, Foster, Wise$bthe Millennium Bridge Project
246.30	$aMillennium Bridge Project
260.00	$aLondon$bAnnely Juda Fine Art$c1998
300.00	$a144 p.$bcol. ill.$c25 cm
500.00	$aCatalogue of an exhibition held at Annely Juda Fine Art, 25 Feb. -18 Apr. 1998
600.10	$aCaro$hAnthony$c1924- $vExhibitions
700.11	$aWise$hChris
710.21	$aSir Norman Foster and Partners
710.21	$aAnnely Juda Fine Art

US MARC

020	$a1870280660
100.1	$aCaro, Anthony,$d1924-
245.10	$aAnthony Caro :$bnew sculptures : a survey: Caro, Foster, Wise : the Millennium Bridge Project.
246.30	$aMillennium Bridge Project.
260	$aLondon :$bAnnely Juda Fine Art,$c1998.
300	$a144 p. :$bcol. ill, ;$c25 cm.
500	$aCatalogue of an exhibition held at Annely Juda Fine Art, 25 Feb. – 18 Apr. 1998.
600.10	$aCaro, Anthony,$d1924- $vExhibitions.
700.1	$aWise, Chris.
710.2	$aSir Norman Foster and Partners.
710.2	$aAnnely Juda Fine Art.

Sample catalogue records

Nicola Hicks
Furtive Imagination

The Whitworth
Art Gallery

This catalogue accompanies the exhibition
Furtive Imagination: Sculpture and Drawings by Nicola Hicks
at the Whitworth Art Gallery, University of Manchester
28 September 1996 - 19 January 1997

Nicola Hicks is represented by Angela Flowers Gallery, London

Title page

Photographs by Edward Woodman
Back cover photograph by Greg Bartley

ISBN 0 903261 33 2

Designed by Epigram
Printed by Philip Myers Press Ltd

Extracted from the last page

UK MARC

021.10	$a0903261332$bm
100.10	$aHicks$hNicola$c1960-
245.10	$aNicola Hicks$bfurtive imagination
246.30	$aFurtive imagination
260.00	$aManchester$bWhitworth Art Gallery$c1997
300.00	$a[16] p.$bill.$c25 cm
500.00	$aCatalogue of an exhibition held at the Whitworth Art Gallery, 28 Sept. 1996-19 Jan. 1997
504.00	$aIncludes bibliographical references
600.10	$aHicks$hNicola$c1960- $vExhibitions
710.21	$aWhitworth Art Gallery

US MARC

020	$a0903261332
100.1	$aHicks, Nicola,$d1960-
245.10	$aNicola Hicks :$bfurtive imagination.
246.30	$aFurtive imagination.
260	$aManchester :$bWhitworth Art Gallery,$c1997.
300	$a[16] p. :$bill. ;$c25 cm.
500	$aCatalogue of an exhibition held at the Whitworth Art Gallery, 28 Sept. 1996-19 Jan. 1997.
504	$aIncludes bibliographical references.
600.10	$aHicks, Nicola,$d1960- $vExhibitions.
710.2	$aWhitworth Art Gallery.

Sample catalogue records

circumstantial evidence

New Works by

TERRY ATKINSON
WILLIE DOHERTY
JOHN GOTO

Texts by

TERRY ATKINSON
JOHN GOTO
DAVID GREEN
PETER SEDDON

University of Brighton 1996

Title page

CIRCUMSTANTIAL EVIDENCE

An exhibition curated by David Green and Peter Seddon.

Published to coincide with the exhibition at the
University of Brighton Gallery, 11-29 November 1996.

Published in an edition of 500 copies.

Texts by Terry Atkinson, John Goto, David Green and Peter Seddon.

© University of Brighton, the artists and authors.

Design, layout and typesetting by Myrene McFee.
Cover design by Myrene McFee.

Extracted from the title page verso

UK MARC

021.10	$a1871966590$bm
100.10	$aAtkinson$hTerry$c1939-
245.10	$aCircumstantial evidence$bnew works by Terry Atkinson, Willie Doherty, John Goto$etexts by Terry Atkinson … [et al.]
260.00	$aBrighton$bUniversity of Brighton$c[1996]
300.00	$a56 p.$bill. (some col.)$c21 x 30 cm
500.00	$a"Published to coincide with the exhibition at the University of Brighton Gallery, 11-29 November 1996" – T.p. verso
504.00	$aIncludes bibliographical references
531.00	$aEdition of 500 copies
600.10	$aAtkinson$hTerry$c1939-$vExhibitions
600.10	$aDoherty$hWillie$c1959-$vExhibitions
600.10	$aGoto$hJohn$c1949-$vExhibitions
700.10	$aDoherty$hWillie$c1959-
700.10	$aGoto$hJohn$c1949-
710.21	$aUniversity of Brighton$cGallery

US MARC

020	$a1871966590
100.1	$aAtkinson, Terry,$d1939-
245.10	$aCircumstantial evidence :$bnew works by Terry Atkinson, Willie Doherty, John Goto /$c texts by Terry Atkinson … [et al.].
260	$aBrighton :$bUniversity of Brighton,$c[1996].
300	$a56 p. :$bill. (some col.) ;$c21 x 30 cm.
500	$a"Published to coincide with the exhibition at the University of Brighton Gallery, 11-29 November 1996" - T.p. verso.
500	$aEdition of 500 copies.
504	$aIncludes bibliographical references.
600.10	$aAtkinson, Terry,$d1939- $vExhibitions.
600.10	$aDoherty, Willie$d1959-$vExhibitions.
600.10	$aGoto, John,$d1949- $vExhibitions.
700.1	$aDoherty, Willie,$d1959-
700.1	$aGoto, John,$d1949-
710.2	$aUniversity of Brighton.$bGallery.

Sample catalogue records

Gwen Raverat
Exhibition

Held at New Hall,
University of Cambridge
13 June - 12 July 1998

Catalogue by Gillie Coutts

By courtesy of the Fitzwilliam Museum

Title page

1000 copies of this catalogue have been printed, of which this is No.

515

ISBN 0 9507108 3 0

© Fitzwilliam Museum and New Hall, University of Cambridge

Published 1998

Extracted from the facing page

UK MARC

021.10	$a095071830$bm
100.10	$aCoutts$hGillie
245.10	$aGwen Raverat exhibition$bheld at New Hall, University of Cambridge, 13 June-12 July 1998$ecatalogue by Gillie Coutts
260.00	$a[Cambridge]$bFitzwilliam Museum$bNew Hall, University of Cambridge$c1998
300.00	$a[48] p.$bill.$iports.$c20 cm
500.00	$aLibrary's copy no. 515
531.00	$aLimited ed. of 1000 numbered copies
600.10	$aRaverat$hGwen$c1885-1957$vExhibitions
700.11	$aRaverat$hGwen$c1885-1957
710.21	$aNew Hall (University of Cambridge)
710.21	$aFitzwilliam Museum

US MARC

020	$a0950710830
100.1	$aCoutts, Gillie.
245.10	$aGwen Raverat exhibition :$bheld at New Hall, University of Cambridge, 13 June-12 July 1998 /$ccatalogue by Gillie Coutts.
260	$a[Cambridge] :$bFitzwilliam Museum ;$aNew Hall, University of Cambridge,$c1998.
300	$a[48] p. :$bill., ports. ;$c20 cm.
500	$aLimited ed. of 1000 numbered copies.
590	$aLibrary's copy no. 515.
600.10	$aRaverat, Gwen,$d1885-1957$vExhibitions.
700.1	$aRaverat, Gwen,$d1885-1957.
710.2	$aNew Hall (University of Cambridge).
710.2	$aFitzwilliam Museum.

APPENDICES

APPENDIX A

ANGLO-AMERICAN CATALOGUING RULES: QUESTIONS AND EXTRACTS

1. How is PROMINENTLY defined?

"The word *prominently* (used in such phrases as *prominently named* and *stated prominently*) means that a statement to which it applies must be a formal statement found in one of the prescribed sources of information ... for areas 1 and 2 for the class of material to which the item being catalogued belongs." – (AACR2 0.8.)

2. What is the PRESCRIBED SOURCE OF INFORMATION?

Each Chapter of AACR2 contains details of a chief source of information for the particular material or publication type covered by the chapter: The chief source for printed books is given below:

"The chief source of information for printed monographs is the title page or, if there is no title page, the source from within the publication that is used as a substitute for it. For printed monographs published without a title page, or without a title page applying to the whole work ..., use the part of the item supplying the most complete information, whether this be the cover (excluding a separate book jacket), caption, colophon, running title, or other part. Specify the part used as a title page substitute in a note ... If no part of the item supplies data that can be used as the basis of the description, take the necessary information from any available source. If the information traditionally given on the title page is given on facing pages or on pages on successive leaves, with or without repetition, treat those pages as the title page...." – (AACR2 2.0B1)

3. How can I identify areas 1 and 2 of the bibliographic description?

The areas of the catalogue description are set out in AACR2 1.0B1:

```
Title and statement of responsibility
Edition
Material (or type of publication) specific details
Publication, distribution, etc.
Physical description
Series
Note
Standard number and terms of availability.
```

Area one is the title and statement of responsibility; area two is the edition

In each subsequent chapters of AACR2 Part I, the section numbering gives the number of the chapter followed by the area number, e.g. 2.1 covers title and statement of responsibility in Chapter 2 Books, Pamphlets and Printed Sheets; 8.1 covers title and statement of responsibility in Chapter 8 Graphic Materials.

4. How is a CORPORATE BODY defined?

"**Definition.** A corporate body is an organization or group of persons that is identified by a particular name and that acts, or may act, as an entity. Consider a corporate body to have a name if the words referring to it are a specific appellation rather than a general description. Consider a body to have a name if, in a script and language using capital letters for proper names, the initial letters of the words referring to it are consistently capitalized, and/or if, in a language using articles, the words are always associated with a definite article. Typical examples of corporate bodies are associations, institutions, business firms, non-profit enterprises, governments, government agencies, projects and programmes, religious bodies, local church groups identified by the name of the church, and conferences.

Some corporate bodies are subordinate to other bodies (e.g., the Peabody Museum of Natural History is subordinate to Yale University; the Annual General Meeting is subordinate to the Canadian Library Association).

Consider ad hoc events (such as athletic contests, exhibitions, expeditions, fairs, and festivals) and vessels (e.g., ships and spacecraft) to be corporate bodies." -(AACR2 21.1B1 Definition)

5. When should CORPORATE BODY be given main entry?

The following extracts are from AACR2 21.1B2:

"**General rule.** Enter a work emanating from one or more corporate bodies under the heading for the appropriate corporate body... if it falls into one or more of the following categories:

a) those of an administrative nature dealing with the corporate body itself
    or its internal policies, procedures, finances, and/or operations
    or its officers, staff, and/or membership (e.g., directories)
    or its resources (e.g., catalogues, inventories)

d) those that report the collective activity of a conference (e.g., proceedings, collected papers), of an expedition (e.g., results of exploration, investigation), **or of an event (e.g., an exhibition, fair, festival) falling within the definition of a corporate body** (see 21.1B1), **provided that the conference, expedition, or event is prominently named (see 0.8) in the item being catalogued.**

6.   What does EMANATE mean?

"Consider a work to emanate from a corporate body if it is issued by that body *or* has been caused to be issued by that body *or* if it originated with that body." - (**AACR2 21.1B2 Footnote 2**)

7.   How do you select the FORM OF NAME for PERSONS?

"In general, choose, as the basis of the heading for a person, the name by which he or she is commonly known. This may be the person's real name, pseudonym, title of nobility, nickname, initials, or other appellation....

Caedmon

D. W. Griffith
not David Wark Griffith

Capability Brown
not Lancelot Brown

H. D.
not Hilda Doolittle

Fra Angelico
not Giovanni da Fiesole
not Guido da Siena

Duke of Wellington
not Arthur Wellesley

William Shakespeare

Jimmy Carter
not James Earl Carter

Anatole France
not Jacques-Anatole Thibault

Giorgione
not Giorgio Barbarelli

Maria Helena
not Maria Helena Vaquinas de Carvalho

John Julius Norwich
not Viscount Norwich

AACR2 22.1A

8. What form should be used when a person CHANGES his or her name?

AACR2 22.2C1 Change of name:

"If a person (other than one using a pseudonym or pseudonyms) has changed his or her name, choose the latest name or form of name unless there is reason to believe that an earlier name will persist as the name by which the person is better known ..."

9. How do you select the FORM OF NAME for CORPORATE BODIES?

"Enter a corporate body directly under the name by which it is commonly identified, except when the rules ... provide for entering it under the name of a higher or related body (see 24.13) " – **(AACR2 24.1A)**

AACR2 24.13 instructs to enter directly unless the name falls within defined categories such as :

Type 1. A name containing a term that by definition implies subordination: e.g. Department, Division, Section, Branch.

Type 3. A name that is general in nature or does no more than indicate a geographic, chronological, or numbered or lettered subdivision of the parent body.

Type 6. A name that includes the entire name of the higher or related body.

10. What form should you use when the Corporate body CHANGES its name?

"If the name of a corporate body has changed (including change from one language to another), establish a new heading under the new name for items appearing under that name. Refer from the old heading to the new and from the new heading to the old (see 26.3C)." **AACR2 24.1C1.**

Note that these extracts are substantially abbreviated. Consult the Anglo-American Cataloguing Rules for full text and examples.

APPENDIX B

USEFUL VOCABULARY IDENTIFYING PUBLICATIONS RELATING TO EXHIBITIONS IN LANGUAGES OTHER THAN ENGLISH:

French: Publié à l'occasion de l'exposition [présentée] à la Galerie.../ au Musée...

            Catalogue d'une exposition présentée ...

German   Erscheint gleichzeitig als Katalog der Austellung ...

            Dieses Buch erschien anlässlich der Austellung ...

            Katalog zur Austellung ...

Italian   Pubblicato in occasione della mostra ...

            Catalogo di una mostra tenuta ...

and words for exhibition / exhibited:

Catalan   exposició; exhibició
Danish   udstilling; fremvisning
Dutch   vertoning; tentoonstelling
Finnish   näyttely
German   Austellung
Hungarian   kiállitás
Italian   mostra; esposizione
Lithuanian   paroda
Norwegian   utstilling; fremvise
Polish   okazanie; wystawa
Portuguese   exposição
Romanian   expozi ie; expunere
Russian   vystavka
Serbo-Croat   izlozba; pokazivanje
Spanish   exposición
Swedish   utställning; utställningsföremål

and **catalogue**:

Catalan   catàleg
Danish   katalog; fortegnelse
Dutch   catalogus
French   catalogue d'exposition
German   Katalog
Hungarian   jegyzék

Italian	catalogo; catalogo d'esposizione; catalogo di mostra
Norwegian	catalog
Polish	katalog; katalog wystawy
Portuguese	catálogo
Russian	katalog
Spanish	catálogo
Swedish	katalog; förteckning; utställningskatalog

APPENDIX C

MAIN ENTRY FOR EXHIBITION CATALOGUES

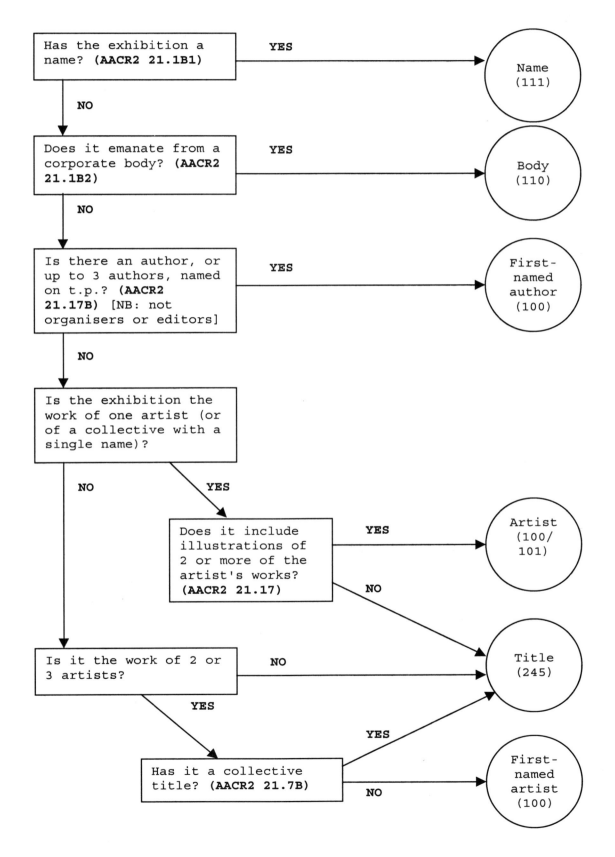

APPENDIX D

CONCORDANCE OF AACR2 RULES AGAINST SECTION AND PAGE NUMBERS

AACR2 Rule	Page reference within Guidelines
0.5	p.41
0.8	p.22, 44, 87, 89
0.29	p.5

Part 1 (Description) p.3, 29, 44 , 87

Part 2 (Headings, Uniform titles, References) p.41

Chapter 1

1.0A1	p.9
1.0B1	p.87
1.0D1	p.5, 24, 32
1.0H	p.51
1.0H1	p.10
1.0H1a)	p.20
1.0H1d)	p.20
1.1	p.3, 11
1.1A2	p.11, 15
1.1B1	p.11, 20
1.1B2	p.14
1.1B3	p.14, 15
1.1B4	p.12, 17
1.1B10	p.19
1.1B20	p.15
1.1C	p.18
1.1C1	p.18
1.1D	p.20
1.1D1	p.20
1.1D3	p.20
1.1D4	p.20
1.1E3	p.12, 17
1.1E5	p.20
1.1F	p.22
1.1F1	p.22
1.1F2	p.22, 24
1.1F3	p.15, 24
1.1F5	p.23

INDEX

accompanying material

    Notes on, 37

    items made up of several types of material, AACR2 1.10C2, 37

       notes on, AACR2 2.7B10, 37

Place names

    added to exhibition name headings, 60-61

Place of publication, distribution, etc., AACR2 1.4C; 26, 27

Plates (printed monographs), AACR2 2.5B10; 29

Posters as catalogues, 30 (*for other rules see* AACR2 Chapter 8 Graphic materials)

Preliminaries

    as sources of information, AACR2 2.0B2; 11, 22, 46

Prescribed sources of information, *see* Sources of information

"Prominently" rules, 22, 44, 87

Proper names, *see* Names

Pseudonyms

    choice of personal name, AACR2 22.2B; 60

Publication date, *see* Date(s) of publication, distribution etc.

Publication, distribution, etc., area, AACR2 1.4; 26

      notes on, AACR2 2.7B9; 36

Publisher, distributor etc., AACR2 1.4D; 26-8

    added entry for publisher as organiser/venue, AACR2 21.30E; 58

    in title and statement of responsibility area, AACR2 1.4D4; 12

Punctuation of description (*see* Parentheses, use of; Square brackets, use of)

Quotation from the item, in notes, 33

Reference sources

    establishing named exhibitions, 44

    for named corporate bodies, definition, AACR2 24.1A2; 44

Reproductions (*see also* Art reproductions)

Rule numbering, explanation, AACR2 0.23; 3, 87

Scope of item, notes on, *see* Nature, scope, or artistic form of item

Series area, AACR2 1.6; 32

Shared authorship, *see* Shared responsibility

Shared pseudonyms, AACR2 21.6D; 60

Single part items with several chief sources of information, AACR2 1.0H1; 10

Size (dimensions), *see* Dimensions

Societies (*for other rules see* Corporate bodies)

    exhibition catalogues emanating from, 47

Source of item, notes on, 37

Source of title proper, notes on, AACR2 1.7B3; 35

Sources of information, AACR2 1.0A; 87

    several chief sources, AACR2 1.0H; 10

Square brackets, use of, 9

Standard number and terms of availability area, AACR2 1.8; 38

Standardization assisted by main entry concept, AACR2 0.5, 41

Statement of extent, *see* Extent, statement of

Statement of publisher, distributor, etc., *see* Publisher, distributor etc.

Statements of responsibility, 22-24

    as part of title proper, AACR2 1.1B2, 1.1F13; 14-17